KNACK™
MAKE IT EASY

CAR CAMP FOR EVERYONE

KNACK™

CAR CAMPING FOR EVERYONE

A Step-by-Step Guide to Planning Your Outdoor Adventure

MARY & BILL BURNHAM

PHOTOGRAPHY BY STEPHEN GORMAN & ELI BURAKIAN

FUELED BY
FALCONGUIDES

KNACK™
MAKE IT EASY

Guilford, Connecticut
An imprint of The Globe Pequot Press

Copyright © 2009 by Morris Book Publishing, LLC

Knack is a registered trademark of Morris Publishing Group, LLC, and is used with express permission.
Falcon and FalconGuides are registered trademarks of Morris Book Publishing, LLC

Editor-in-Chief: Maureen Graney
Editor: Katie Benoit
Cover Design: Paul Beatrice, Bret Kerr
Text Design: Paul Beatrice
Layout: Kevin Mak
Cover photos by Stephen Gorman
Interior photos by Stephen Gorman with the exception of Photos p. xii (left): Monkey Business Images/shutterstock; p. xii right: Gene Chutka/istockphoto; p. 1 (right): istockphoto; p. 2 (right): Ronald Sherwood/shutterstock; p. 4 (left): Ryan Howe/istockphoto; p. 7 (left): © Magda Moiola | Dreamstime.com; p. 7 (right): XAOC/shutterstock; p. 8 (right): © Rafa Irusta | Dreamstime.com; p. 11 (right): Courtesy of Kelty; p. 12 (left): Courtesy of Big Agnes; p. 12 (right): Courtesy of Big Agnes; p. 13 (left): Courtesy of Coleman; p. 13 (right): Courtesy of Coleman; p. 23 (right): Courtesy of Coleman; p. 55 (right): © Andy Heyward | Dreamstime.com; p. 71 (left): Flashon Studio/shutterstock; p. 71 (right): Judy Foldetta/istockphoto; p. 72 (right): Steve Shepard/istockphoto; p. 79 (right): Courtesy of Eureka; p. 82 (left): BurnhamInk.com; p. 90 (right): © Nicolette Neish | Dreamstime.com; p. 91 (left): © Nicolette Neish | Dreamstime.com; p. 91 (right): © Emmanuel Lacoste | Dreamstime.com; p. 97 (right): © 2006 Weber-Stephen Products Co. Used with permission; p. 103 (right): © David Coleman | Dreamstime.com; p. 108 (right): © Ashley Whitworth | Dreamstime.com; p. 112 (right): Toos van den Dikkenberg/istockphoto; p. 113 (left): Sascha Burkard/shutterstock; p. 113 (right): photos.com; p. 114 (right): Jonathan Davies/istockphoto; p. 115 (right): © Smphoto | Dreamstime.com; p. 119 (right): ncn18/shutterstock; p. 120 (left): © Brightdawn | Dreamstime.com; p. 121 (left): Allister Clark/istockphoto; p. 121 (right): Clint Spencer/istockphoto; p. 125 (left): © Ron Chapple Studios | Dreamstime.com; p. 125 (right): Laura Eisenberg/istockphoto; p. 126 (left): Iurii Konoval/shutterstock; p. 126 (right): ryasick/shutterstock; p. 127 (left): Laurie Knight/istockphoto; p. 127 (right): © Elisalocci | Dreamstime.com; p. 128 (left): sabrina dei nobili/istockphoto; p. 128 (right): © Kobby Dagan | Dreamstime.com; p. 129 (left): Clint Spencer/istockphoto; p. 129 (right): © Nico Smit | Dreamstime.com; p. 130 (left): © Johnbell | Dreamstime.com; p. 130 (right): Suzann Julien/istockphoto; p. 131 (left): Scott Winegarden/istockphoto; p. 131 (right): John Pitcher/istockphoto; p. 136 (right): Sebastian Kaulitzki/istockphoto; p. 137 (right): © Shhaase | Dreamstime.com; p. 143 (left): Leah-Anne Thompson/istockphoto; p. 143 (right): Sharon Dominick/istockphoto; p. 146 (left): Stuart Monk/shutterstock; p. 146 (right): Artem Efimov/shutterstock; p. 147 (left): Artem Efimov/shutterstock; p. 148 (left): Andrzej Szałapata/istockphoto; p. 148 (right): istockphoto; p. 149 (left): © Klevo | Dreamstime.com; p. 151 (left): © Sebastian Czapnik | Dreamstime.com; p. 153 (right): Lisa Valder/istockphoto; p. 156 (left): istockphoto; p. 156 (right): Courtesy of Coleman; p. 158 (left): B.G. Smith/shutterstock; p. 166 (left): BurnhamInk.com; p. 166 (right): istockphoto; p. 176 (left): Alessandro Contadini/istockphoto; p. 178 (left): Christophe Testi/shutterstock; p. 178 (right): Jacek Chabraszewski/shutterstock; p. 179 (left): Jeanette Zehentmayer/istockphoto; p. 180 (left): © Monica Minford | Dreamstime.com; p. 180 (right): © Mike Rogal | Dreamstime.com; p. 181 (left): © Sascha Burkard | Dreamstime.com; p. 182 (left): John Pitcher/istockphoto; p. 182 (right): Richard Fitzer/shutterstock; p. 183 (left): © Terry Reimink | Dreamstime.com; p. 183 (right): © Outdoorsman | Dreamstime.com; p. 184 (left): © Albert Trujillo | Dreamstime.com; p. 184 (right): Ronnie Howard/shutterstock; p. 185 (left): © Bruce Macqueen | Dreamstime.com; p. 185 (right): James Coleman/shutterstock; p. 186 (right): Steve Byland/shutterstock; p. 187 (left): © Norman Bateman | Dreamstime.com; p. 187 (right): sonya etchison/shutterstock; p. 188 (left): © David Park | Dreamstime.com; p. 188 (right): © Rusty Dodson | Dreamstime.com; p. 189 (left): © Lloyd Luecke | Dreamstime.com; p. 189 (right): © Charles Lytton | Dreamstime.com; p. 190 (left): Courtesy of Home Science Tools; p. 190 (right): © Gregg Williams | Dreamstime.com; p. 191 (left): Eric Michaud/istockphoto; p. 191 (right): ahnhuynh/shutterstock; p. 203 (right): Falk Kienas/shutterstock

Library of Congress Cataloging-in-Publication Data is available on file.

ISBN 978-1-59921-505-1

The following manufacturers/names appearing in *Knack Car Camping* are trademarks:
Bisquick®, CamelBak®, Camp Chef®, Crazy Creek Products®, Crocs™, Frisbee®, GORE-TEX®, GORP®, Hamburger Helper®, Kellogg's® Rice Krispies®, Leatherman®, Monopoly®, Oreos™, Polarguard®, REI®, Sierra Trading Post®, Thermos®, Thinsulate™, Velcro®

The information in this book is true and complete to the best of our knowledge. All recommendations are made without guarantee on the part of the author or The Globe Pequot Press. The author and The Globe Pequot Press disclaim any liability in connection with the use of this information.

Printed in China

10 9 8 7 6 5 4 3 2 1

Dedicated to our 16 (and counting) nieces and nephews

Acknowledgments

We'd like thank our parents, who were brave enough to take family car camping trips as soon as their kids could walk (or earlier)!

Bill's family of nine camped in a huge teepee that his dad towed on a trailer behind the station wagon to lakes in upstate New York's Adirondack Mountains. Mary's family also tented on some of the same Adirondack lakes. Little did they realize they'd meet someday and start a lifetime of camping together all across the country.

Here's to the next generation: our nieces and nephews, many of whom we've 'borrowed' to take camping and backpacking through the years. The older ones are now camping on their own. The younger ones we hope to someday introduce to all the joys of camping we've known.

CONTENTS

INTRODUCTION:
Roads Less Traveled

After more than a decade of camping and several stints living out of our car for months on end, it's not a stretch to say we have car camping nailed down. Once we complete one trip, planning for the next one is already brewing in our minds. Our gear is always packed, our supplies stocked, and we've even designated a spare bedroom as the gear room. Each box, pack, food tub, and duffel bag has a place in our car.

But this wasn't always so. Starting with our very first trip as a young couple, we learned by trial and error. Our first full day of driving down the East Coast ended at a campground on the James River near Williamsburg. The campsite on a bluff overlooking the river was idyllic. We

immediately grabbed two lawn chairs from our car and sat transfixed, watching a Great Blue Heron wade along the streamside. Later, a kingfisher zipped from one tree to another with its characteristic chatter. The sun set, and shadows crept across the campsite.

It was then that we turned to one another, realizing our tent wasn't up yet, and, as if on cue, said, "Now what?"

The frustration of setting up camp in the dark taught us (over time) to pack efficiently. In the beginning, we forgot important items, like tent poles. We took unnecessary items, like lawn chairs. And more often than not, the car was a chaotic mess, making it difficult to find anything quickly. On our first long trip, a three-month journey around the United States, we regularly shipped home useless gear — or even gave it away. Only through time and tips from more experienced friends did we become a stream-lined car camping machine.

So why do we go through all this effort to camp? Imagine, if you will, waking up and unzipping the tent door, staring out upon the craggy, snow-capped peaks of Washington's Olympic Range. Consider pitching a tent at the bottom of a Wyoming canyon, in a North Carolina swamp, or in the middle of a prehistoric lava flow in New Mexico. We've experienced wild ponies nosing about our tent tucked in dunes of a Maryland barrier island. We've perched ourselves on colorful cliffs overlooking Michigan's Lake Superior and at the brink of the Grand Tetons.

We've woken up on an island paradise in the Florida Keys, and set up camp on a Minnesota tallgrass prairie.

Our love of camping motivates us to toss gear into the car, spur of the moment, and drive to a deserted beach campsite on Assateague Island, or to a pristine mountain lake in southwest Virginia, or to our favorite Florida Keys campsites.

And these are just a sampling of places we've found since we caught the car camping bug over sixteen years ago. For us, it's the love and awe of the outdoors that constantly draws us back out there.

We want to share this love of car camping with you. It doesn't matter whether you've never camped before or haven't camped since your childhood. *Knack Car Camp-*

zero impact on the land as you camp, hike, and explore your environment. Enjoy new games to play with the family. Follow the photographs and sidebars scattered throughout for efficient ways of organizing and packing gear, setting up camp, cooking, and cleaning.

And, most importantly, unleash your love for the outdoors. Make it your goal to leave as much time for playing in and enjoying the outdoors as possible. Camping, after all, is fun, and this book aims to prove just that.

Sharing with children, for example, the joy of discovery in the outdoors—finding a frog in a small mountain stream or soaking in unforgettable views off a towering cliff after a hard climb—motivates us to make sure that, in addition to whatever practical information you glean from this book, you discover the joy of sharing quality time with family and friends outdoors.

ing For Everyone visually distills our practical knowledge into one easy-to-read guide. We give you the tools to overcome challenges like weather, insects, safety, cleanliness, or boredom on rainy days. Even those with experience will find something new here. Car camping can also lead to other outdoor adventure treats—fishing, hunting, boating, horseback riding, or bird-watching—and we touch upon those pursuits in these pages, as well.

Knack Car Camping For Everyone addresses solo minimalist campers; families with children, older generations, and pets; and the comfort camper for whom roughing it is not an option. Our goal is to make camping accessible for all, even those on a tight budget.

Because, as it should, planning turns into acting, we offer advice on surmounting all challenges. Learn what to bring, and what to leave at home. Discover ways to have

The excitement that grips us as we pull away from our home and embark on a car camping trip is as strong today as it was when we took our first trip. Sure, we may be a little more organized now and may no longer pack our lawn chairs, but the rush we felt that first time we set up camp greets us every time we step foot in a new campground.

WHO IS GOING?

This decision will affect many others: destination, trip length, and gear

There's no greater bonding experience than delving into nature with friends and family. That's the basis—and continuing sustenance—of many of our friendships.

That said, deciding whom to take on your camping trip is not something to rush into.

The most beautiful destination in the world can be soured if people aren't getting along, or if one person in the group is having a miserable time.

Know the members of your group well, their abilities, fitness, threshold for "roughing it," and personality quirks. That goes double for the family pet! First, be sure the campground allows pets, but also consider your dog's temperament.

Family Camping

- How young is too young? Many doctors advise waiting until about six months of age, when baby can sit up on its own, but experienced camping families start in infancy.

- Consider all you'll need to bring: playpens, carriers, bikes, and games.

- Engage children in all aspects of the trip: planning, camp set-up, and cooking.

- A family camping vacation is a great opportunity to unplug. Consider leaving the handheld music and gaming devices at home, and listening to birds and gazing at stars instead.

Multi-generational

- Grandparents are often great storytellers. Encourage them to share their experiences around the fire.

- Skills like fishing, birdwatching, and canoeing are skills that the older generation can pass along to youngsters.

- Don't forget the still camera or video camera. You might even consider a tape recorder to document family history.

- Do take into account any mobility issues in the group, and be sure anyone on medications brings along those medications.

Ease first-time campers, whatever their age, into the outdoors by choosing a campground with lots of amenities, and perhaps starting with a quick overnight.

Young children are often delighted in the most basic aspects of nature—it's all new to them! Be on the lookout for fun teaching moments at every turn.

Teens may require more excitement and structured activities. Schedule in a paintball game or whitewater rafting to keep them engaged. The rewards of a multi-generational trip are long-lasting memories.

Grandma and Grandpa may not mind sleeping in a tent if they have a good air mattress or cot. Or they may opt to bring their camper or stay in a cabin nearby. Everyone can come together for an evening barbecue and chat around the fire. A campground with varied options is a great location for a family vacation or reunion that will make everyone comfortable.

Scout and youth group trips come with a whole other level of challenges. You'll need a boatload of patience and a big "bag of tricks." But such experiences can be something kids will remember for the rest of their lives.

Bring the Dog?

- Be sure to check ahead to find out if pets are allowed in the campground, how many are allowed, and if there's a weight limit.

- Wildlife refuges seldom allow dogs, but many state park campgrounds do.

- Consider how your dog reacts to strangers, other dogs, and wildlife and plan accordingly.

- Cats aren't normally great travelers, but there are exceptions. Just be sure yours doesn't get loose.

Scout and Youth Groups

- Youth group camping areas, set apart from the main public area, often have their own rules and regulations. Check them in advance.

- The recommended adult-to-youth ratio is at least one adult per ten campers under eighteen years old.

- You'll need to get some important paperwork from the parents, including permission to get the kids medical treatment.

- You should be trained in basic first aid, at the least. Scouting organizations require leaders to be trained and certified.

WHERE TO GO
There are millions of camping options on public and private lands

Those with a high threshold for uncertainty might not mind spontaneous trips, simply throwing everything in the car, hitting the road, and trusting they'll find a spot to camp. Most of us like to know where we'll be resting our heads, so some planning is required and usually a campground reservation.

First, decide how long you want to be in the car. Are you looking forward to a real adventure, going someplace you've never been before? Then you might not mind driving a day or two to reach one of our nation's treasures.

Or is an hour quite long enough for the little ones who'll be accompanying you? There may be a perfectly good state park with a swimming lake near your home city. The U.S. has many millions of acres of public land, most of it open to recreation. Public campgrounds—national, state, or county—

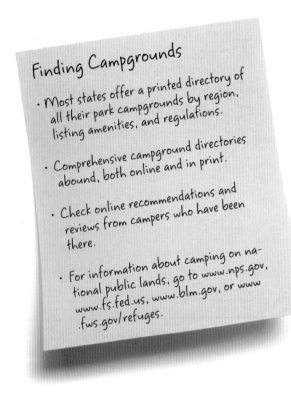

Finding Campgrounds
- Most states offer a printed directory of all their park campgrounds by region, listing amenities, and regulations.
- Comprehensive campground directories abound, both online and in print.
- Check online recommendations and reviews from campers who have been there.
- For information about camping on national public lands, go to www.nps.gov, www.fs.fed.us, www.blm.gov, or www.fws.gov/refuges.

Public versus Private

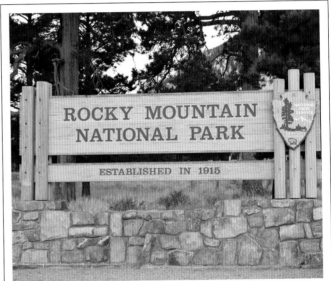

- Public parks: National and state parks typically have excellent campgrounds with many amenities.

- Public lands: National forests, wildlife refuges, and Bureau of Land Management campgrounds may have fewer amenities but usually cost less and offer a true wilderness experience.

- Private campgrounds, vary tremendously. Research well.

- Events: Camping may be offered at music festivals, car races, and other events. Be sure the event is appropriate for your family.

are typically clean, well run, and consistent.

Private campgrounds, like any type of establishment, vary greatly in quality, price, and management. Go to their websites, read online reviews, call to ask questions, and gauge their friendliness. You just may find a well-run mom-and-pop or chain franchise campground that you'll return to year after year.

Event camping, at music festivals, car races, or motorcycle races, can be a blast. Just be sure you know the atmosphere before you go. Alcohol, drugs, even nudity might be present. Large crowds often lead to dirty bathrooms and noisy nights!

GREEN ● LIGHT

Know the rules before you go. Are you allowed to build a fire? Hang a clothesline? Consume alcohol? Reserve enough space; campgrounds usually limit the number of tents, people, pets, and vehicles per site and may charge an additional fee for extra people or pets. Find out the campground's quiet hours and posted speed limit. Ask about bears. In areas with high bear interaction, there may be a fine for leaving out food or trash.

Amenities and Services

- Full hook-ups: These sites are usually for RVs, but you may want the convenience of water and electric in your site. They are often close to the bathhouse.

- Other features: There may be a bear hook for hanging food, a clothesline, or a cooking grill.

- Campground amenities: Some campgrounds are outdoor resorts, with pools, marinas, and restaurants on-site. At the least, a self-service laundry and a recreation room for rainy days are nice to have.

Rustic Sites

- Some tent areas may have a picnic table and fire ring, but tent areas are often more secluded and quiet.

- Some campgrounds have walk-in sites that require you to carry your gear to the site. There may be a portable toilet nearby rather than a bathhouse.

- These areas often bring the reward of a true outdoor experience, like a tent spot right on the beach.

- Camping in a primitive site means you should know the proper way to dispose of wastewater and protect food from wildlife.

GREAT DESTINATIONS
Lakes, forests, beaches, and peaks create memorable experiences

Picture this: Carrying steaming mugs of morning coffee, you walk from your campsite down to the white sand beach that stretches as far as the eye can see. In nearby dunes, a wild pony noses around beach scrub, looking for breakfast. But your eyes are focused 200 yards offshore, watching a pod of dolphins arching and jumping in single file. Around you, tiny terns play cat-and-mouse with the waves.

Such are the rewards of camping on a barrier island beach, in this case Maryland's Assateague Island. But our nation's lakes, forests, and mountains provide equally inspiring camping experiences. Even if you camp with the family vehicle, you don't have to leave adventure behind. You'll be surprised by the places you can get to and pitch tent—and you won't even need four-wheel drive.

Lakeside

- Camp on a pristine northern lake where your wake-up call is the cry of a loon.

- Choose a little more action on a recreational lake with waterskiing, boating, and fishing.

- Some favorite lakeside camping spots include

Adirondack State Park, upstate New York; Pictured Rocks National Lakeshore, Michigan's Upper Peninsula; Lake Powell's beaches and canyons, Utah.

- Bring canoes or kayaks and fishing poles to take full advantage of lakeside camping.

Mountain View

- Breathtaking mountain vistas and peaks await at these favorites:

- Campgrounds in Virginia's Shenandoah National Park are perched atop the Blue Ridge Mountains.

- You'll feel like you're camping in the clouds at Olympic National Park in Washington.

- Camp beside the dramatic vertical rise of the Grand Tetons in Wyoming.

Making a pilgrimage to our national treasures—Yosemite, Yellowstone, Grand Tetons, the Grand Canyon, the Maine Coast—is something every camper will want to attempt at least once in life.

But even if you have only a weekend or a quick overnight, you'll find that rewarding experiences await at your nearby state or county park. Perhaps it's a quiet spot on a pristine Adirondack lake or a deep woods site in a national forest in Virginia.

GREEN ● LIGHT

When camping in environmentally sensitive areas like alpine, desert, or beach, be sure to follow Leave No Trace practices as well as any specific regulations of the local campground (see Resources). Fires may not be allowed on the beach, for instance, and in areas above the tree line, you must be extra careful of fragile vegetation.

Beach Sites

- There are many special places in the U.S. where you can pitch your tent right on the beach. Here are some favorites:

- On East Coast beaches, you can watch the sun rise over the Atlantic at places like Assateague Island National Seashore, Maryland.

- On the West Coast, watch it set over the Pacific at Redwood National and State Parks, California.

- The Florida Keys are a special island paradise where you can watch the sun rise on one side of an island and set on the other. Bahia Honda State Park is a favorite.

Crossing Borders

- If you'll be crossing into Canada or Mexico, you'll need identification and proof of citizenship to return.

- A passport, passport card, or trusted traveler card will do.

- Without the above, you may need both identification (state driver's license) and proof of citizenship (birth certificate).

- Be sure everyone, including children, has these documents.

- For more information, visit travel.state .gov.

WHEN TO GO

Consider peak seasons, weather, and climate in choosing a time to camp

There are two ways to plan when to go camping: pick your destination and figure out the best time for camping there or pick your dates first and find a good spot.

The "shoulder seasons"—in spring before Memorial Day or in autumn after Labor Day—are nice times to avoid crowds and humidity. But be prepared for winter weather to spill over into either one. It's not uncommon to be unexpectedly snowed on in both April and October in Virginia's mountains, for example.

Of course, if you're locked into the kids' summer vacation, you don't have much choice. So you'll want to research what the crowds will be like during the peak season, especially in popular national parks.

Top Ten Most Visited National Parks:
(Based on 2007 Statistics)
- Great Smoky Mountains
- Grand Canyon
- Yosemite
- Yellowstone
- Olympic
- Rocky Mountain
- Zion
- Grand Teton
- Cuyahoga Valley
- Acadia

Camping Seasons

- Spring: Wildflowers blooming and refreshing temps. Be prepared for cold nights and the occasional late snowfall.

- Summer: The most popular time to camp in most parts of the country. In warmer climates, it can be muggy and buggy.

- Autumn: Leaf-peeping, bird migrations, and cooler temps.

- Winter: Peak season in Florida and other southern states. Most people avoid winter camping in colder climes, but that's just the point.

Climate and local weather patterns are also considerations. Humidity and mosquitoes can make sleeping in a tent a miserable experience. Hurricane season and localized severe weather are other factors to consider.

Festivals, music events, and sporting events are other destinations around which to plan a trip. Animal and bird migrations and flower and foliage displays are others. Unless you're a hunter, hunting season is a time you should avoid being in the woods.

YELLOW ● LIGHT

Consider the weather: Use the Internet to check monthly temperature and precipitation averages in advance. Check the weather and radar right before you head out for any severe weather coming. Consider getting a weather band radio (some car radios now offer it) to check for severe weather alerts that develop while on your trip. For coastal camping, remember that Atlantic hurricane season runs June 1 through November 30, and the Pacific hurricane season begins May 15.

Look for large sites with natural buffers.

Peter Season *Peak Season*

- Try to schedule your trip to avoid peak seasons at popular national parks.

- If possible, go mid-week during peak seasons.

- Online reservation systems (like reservations.nps.gov or reserveamerica.com) allow booking up to eleven months in advance. This is a must at the most popular national parks and state parks in the Florida Keys.

- The National Recreation Reservation Service (recreation.gov) allows you to book up to six months in advance.

Avoiding Crowds

- Of course, if you are taking the kids on summer vacation, and you want them to experience the top natural landmarks, it will be difficult to avoid peak season.

- Choose campgrounds and sites that have natural features like trees and topography to provide some privacy.

- Another option is to avoid the national parks and choose private, forest service, or Bureau of Land Management campgrounds.

- These may be less crowded but afford access to the same natural wonders.

MINIMALIST CAMPING

Keep it simple to have as little as possible between you and nature

What's your camping style? Are you a minimalist or a "bring the kitchen sink" camper? Determining your group's threshold for roughing it will keep everyone happy and comfortable.

Camping style has a big impact on the type of gear you'll want to acquire, so decide early on to save time and money.

If you ever anticipate going backpacking—strapping everything onto your back and hitting the trail—choose gear that is lightweight yet can double for car camping. Kayak, canoe, or bike camping also requires minimal, lightweight gear.

Or perhaps you simply want the option of a walk-in primitive campsite offered at many developed campgrounds to give you a backwoods experience. In all of these cases, you need to purchase gear accordingly and pack it efficiently.

Minimalist Gear List

• Two- or three-person domed tent

• Sleeping bags and roll-up pads

• Single-burner stove

• Lightweight, nesting cookware

• Individual mess kits

Going Off-road

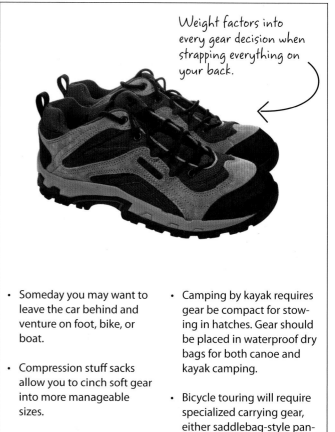

Weight factors into every gear decision when strapping everything on your back.

• Someday you may want to leave the car behind and venture on foot, bike, or boat.

• Compression stuff sacks allow you to cinch soft gear into more manageable sizes.

• Camping by kayak requires gear be compact for stowing in hatches. Gear should be placed in waterproof dry bags for both canoe and kayak camping.

• Bicycle touring will require specialized carrying gear, either saddlebag-style panniers or a trailer.

Resist the temptation to go on a spending spree. Outdoor catalogs, stores, and websites are chock full with all kinds of fancy gear and gizmos. As clever as it looks, do you really need that portable espresso maker? Decide ahead what you really need, and take a list.

Domed backpacking-style tents are lightweight and usually easy to set up.

The Tent

- Even though you're camping light, sleeping comfortably is important.

- There are some items you simply can't improvise. A good tent is one. The right decision now will keep you warm and dry for many years to come.

- The lightest backpacking tents weigh only a couple of pounds. Try to keep it under ten pounds.

- Choose inexpensive, roll-up sleeping pads, sleeping bags that stuff compactly, and either inflatable or stuffable pillows.

Single-burner Stove

- Choose a single-burner stove with a refillable fuel container or a propane canister.

- Some micro-canister stoves feature an attached mug for boiling water.

- Nesting pots with foldable handles are very easy to

pack. Choose inexpensive aluminum or stainless steel, or invest in superlight titanium.

- Mess kits for individual tableware also save space. The good old kinds that the Boy Scouts use are fine. Or simply grab extra plates, mugs, and utensils from the kitchen.

COMFORT CAMPING
Camping doesn't have to mean roughing it

Is a member of your party a nervous first-timer or a reluctant camper because he or she remembers uncomfortable camping trips from childhood?

There's a lot available these days to make camping a complete pleasure. The products available, from supercomfortable mattresses to portable espresso machines, can make your head spin.

The campsite is truly your home away from home, so create a homey atmosphere with a tablecloth, comfortable folding chairs, and a large cooler to always keep ice-cold drinks handy. Battery-operated, solar, or hand-cranked fans, radios, and even televisions are available as well.

And for the camp gourmet, elaborate cooking stations include four-burner propane stoves, prep space, and shelves.

Comfort Gear List

• Inflatable mattress

• Down sleeping bags

• Folding chairs

• Screen room

• Percolator

Cushy Tent

A silk sleeping bag liner adds a touch of luxury and keeps bags cleaner.

• To sleep as well in the woods as you do at home, a comfortable mattress is key.

• Good inflatable mattresses, the kind with the pump attached, are as comfortable as any mattress and come in queen and king sizes.

• Invest in down sleeping

bags: They're the most comfortable, and the kind that zip together make a cozy nest for two.

• Bring something to read at bedtime and either a headlamp or a small battery-operated lantern.

• Don't forget the pillows!

Hey, why not throw in that hand-cranked blender for some frozen margaritas? For some campers, if it fits in the vehicle, they'll bring it!

Staying warm and dry is a key to comfortable camping. Invest in a good rain suit—jacket and pants—rather than relying on a cheap poncho. Hikers will find clothes of quick-drying wicking material more comfortable than cotton. If there's any chance of colder weather, plan to bring high-performance clothes that can be layered.

ZOOM

Add color and style to your campsite sitting area with an outdoor area rug. Weatherproof rugs come in all colors and even Oriental patterns! It may sound like the ultimate in luxury, but it has practical aspects as well, providing a clean space for children to play.

Spread Out

- A large tent feels luxurious and provides room for the comforts of home.

- Cabin tents are large enough to stand up in and can accommodate cots, cribs, and gear.

- Some have a removable privacy partition to create two rooms. Even if it rains all day, there's room to stretch out with a good book.

- Heck, bring the bean bag chairs and battery-operated TV!

Gourmet Kitchen

- Bring what you need for gourmet meals in the woods.

- Two-, three-, or four-burner camping stoves stand up to most tests.

- Bring a deluxe cookware set and the utensils you need,

whether you're making kebabs or crepes. Create, or buy, a spice kit.

- A collapsible, two-sided sink will enable clean-ups right at your site.

TENTS BY DESIGN
This may be the most important gear decision you will make

Today's tents come in numerous styles and sizes, from one-person bivy sacks to eight-person family cabins. When camping, your tent is your castle, so choose wisely to keep everyone happy, comfortable, and dry.

If you ever think you'll go backpacking, weight will be the key issue. The tent should be well under ten pounds. Consider who will carry it, or split up the components among two people. In general, buy the lightest tent that will meet your needs.

Our first tent choice was based on an experienced friend's recommendation: a three-season, three-person Sierra Designs Meteor Light. Considering we're still using it more than ten years later, for both backpacking and car camping, at under $300, it was a terrific investment.

There are plenty of ways to make do with older or repur-

Solo Minimalist

- The freewheeling camper is just as likely to throw gear into a backpack as the car on a moment's notice.

- In order of ascending roominess, choose an enclosed hammock, a mummy-shaped bivy shelter (pictured), or a one-person hoop tent. The latter will give you the most head room and possibly a vestibule.

- Pros: One-person shelters are lightweight, and set-up is quick and easy.

- Cons: You can't invite company, and Fido will have to sleep outside.

Couple on the Go

- A dome tent is perfect for a cozy couple or a small family with one or two little ones.

- Count the members of your group, then bump up the total by one. The typical "two-person" is more comfortable for one. A "three-person" is better for two bodies, some gear, a small child, or a dog.

- Pros: Dome tents are the most stable in high winds, freestanding, and usually have a good rain fly (the canvas flap at the entrance of the tent) and vestibule.

- Cons: None!

posed camping gear in order to save some money, but the tent is not one of them. The first time you wake up swimming in your tent, or the zipper gets stuck with hungry mosquitoes trying to get in, or a tent pole breaks in the dark, you'll be convinced of that!

Take your time and do your research. Start with the Internet and outdoor catalogs. Try to get to an outdoor store where you can get inside of and lie down in a number of tents. Consider renting from an outfitter or borrowing from a friend to try out different styles.

ZOOM

Tent shapes: The A-frame tent is the oldest design. It has a simple structure and is easy to put up but is not very sturdy. The tunnel frame uses two curved poles to increase headroom. The dome frame uses two or three curved poles that cross for additional stability. Wall or cabin frames are more like the room of a house—more space but harder to put up.

Family Vacation

- Cabin tents are large and square, can accommodate cots, crib, gear, and larger families.

- Some have a removable partition to create two rooms for privacy.

- Pros: You can stand up inside, which makes changing clothes easier. Even if it rains all day, there's room to stretch out with a good book or a game of cards.

- Cons: Cabin tents take longer to set up than dome tents.

Taj Mahal

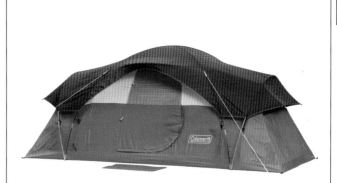

- Larger families may have teenagers and perhaps grandparents along for a week in the woods, so this tent is a good option.

- These "tent condos" should have at least two doors and plenty of storage pockets and loops inside for hanging things.

- Pros: There's tons of room. Heck, bring the bean bag chairs and battery-operated TV.

- Cons: They're heavy and take some time to put up. Also, consider the space the tent will take up in your car.

TENTS BY SEASON

Have a clear idea of the kind of weather you'll be camping in most often when picking your tent

The days of the heavy, moldy, leaky, canvas tent are long gone. Today's tents are made from superior materials that are lightweight and resist moisture. Tents are designed to protect you from wind, rain, and cold as well as critters and bugs.

In addition to the number of people they hold, tents are categorized according to the season or weather conditions they can be used in: summer, three-season, or winter (four-season).

They vary in material, stability, and weight and generally go up in cost from summer to winter.

Think carefully about the conditions you'll be camping in *most often*, but be prepared for surprises. We know from personal experience that it can snow in Virginia in April. Hence,

Sleeping Out in the Open

- Some campers believe sleeping al fresco is the epitome of camping. But do check the campground rules: Some don't permit camping without a tent.

- Check the weather report, too! If there's a chance of showers, you can set up a tarp to sleep under.

- Pros: Simplicity, low-cost, and awesome stargazing.

- Cons: Bugs and critters. Consider mosquito netting, and be sure there's no food or trash around to attract raccoons, skunks, or bears.

Lightweight Summer Tent

- A summer-rated tent is fine for those who live in a warm climate or plan on camping only in fair weather.

- The tent body has lots of mesh for maximum ventilation and stargazing on clear nights.

- Pro: Summer tents are light-weight and easy to put up.

- Con: They are not as sturdy as three-season tents, and there can always be an occasional cool night, even in summer.

the three-season tent is best if you plan on camping during any time but summer.

A summer tent may be fine if you live in a warm climate or intend on camping only in fair weather. But in higher elevations, even summer can be chilly, and southern climates are notorious for quick-forming, strong thunderstorms.

Be sure you really and truly need to invest the extra money (and weight) in a winter or four-season tent. Also known as "expedition tents," these are built to handle the most extreme conditions in northern climates and high altitudes.

MAKE IT EASY

Choose a tent that is easy and quick to set up, in case you arrive after dark or there's a monsoon coming. If possible, try to set up a tent in the store before purchasing it. After purchase, practice set-up and take-down in your backyard or living room.

Three-Season Tent

Winter Tent

- A three-season tent is perfect if you don't want to be locked in to a particular season, terrain, or region. Look for the freestanding kind and a rain fly that comes down to the ground.

- Three-season tents are the most versatile and quite adequate for most weather conditions you'll encounter spring through autumn.

- Pros: Mesh fabric allows for ventilation, while sturdy construction can withstand moderate winds and even light snowfalls.

- Cons: None!

- Winter tents, or four-season tents, are designed to withstand the most severe conditions of high winds, heavy snowfall, and cold temperatures.

- These tents have extra strong poles and storm windows, and some have even a condensation sponge to collect moisture and keep the rain fly from touching the tent body.

- Pro: You'll sleep cozy and secure, no matter what Mother Nature throws at you.

- Con: These tents are heavy and typically not well ventilated.

TENT FEATURES
Details make a big difference in comfort level and use

Most tents today are made of nylon or polyester fabrics that protect from the wind and rain while remaining breathable.

Look for double-wall construction: an inner, breathable tent with mesh for ventilation and an outer rain fly. The rain fly and the tent floor should be coated or laminated with a waterproof material like polyurethane or GORE-TEX.

Seams should be double-stitched with two rows of stitch-ing for strength. Rip-stop fabric will prevent small tears from getting worse.

Most tent poles today are made of aluminum alloy tubing: strong but lightweight. Carbon fiber is even better but is used in more expensive, technical tents. Avoid fiberglass poles that come with cheaper tents. Fiberglass is not as strong, so thicker, heavier poles are required. It's preferable for dome

Ventilation

- Tents get stuffy, especially in warm weather, so ventilation is key for optimal sleeping.

- Look for large mesh windows and partial roof for ventilation.

- A roof that's mostly mesh means that on a clear, dry night you can leave the rain fly off and stargaze as you fall asleep.

- If you decide to sleep sans rain fly, be sure to keep it nearby by just in case you feel sprinkles and need to put it on in a hurry.

Interior Features

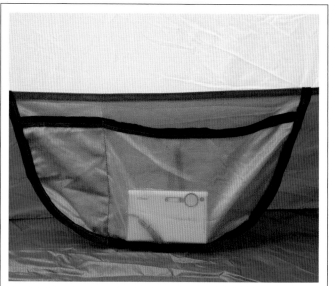

- Look for a bathtub floor: The waterproof floor material meets the wall several inches from the ground to protect from groundwater.

- Inside pockets are handy to stash bedtime essentials like car keys, cell phone, flashlight, bug spray, and tissues.

- Look for pockets at both ends of the tent so you can sleep either way.

- Loops for hanging a flashlight or air freshener are a nice detail.

tents to have three poles rather than two for more stability in wind. Poles that cross each other provide even more rigidity.

Pole sleeves are a nice feature. You run the pole through the sleeve sewn on the inner tent to distribute strain evenly. Poles may also be attached by clips that snap on easily. Many tents will use a combination of both styles.

Today's tent makers try hard to make it easy: Some tents have poles and grommets color-coded for quick set-up.

ZOOM

A lighter-colored tent fabric—pale blue, yellow, or tan—will let in more natural light and remain cooler in warm climates. Darker-colored tents will absorb more heat: better for cold climates.

Vestibule

- A vestibule provides an anteroom for dirty boots and gear (or even a dog!) while keeping them dry.

- Right before bedtime, do a sweep of the campsite to see if there's anything you don't want to get wet.

- Even if there's no rain forecast, nighttime condensation can drench your gear.

- It's nice for doors to have a two-way zipper so you can open it from either side.

Rain Fly

- Choose a tent with a rain fly that comes down to within a few inches of the ground.

- This will prevent wind-driven rain from entering your tent enclosure.

- The rain fly is usually attached to the base of the tent by clip buckles.

- The rain fly often extends off the tent to form the vestibule. Look for loops and fasteners that allow the outer door to be rolled up for ventilation.

TENT ACCESSORIES
Like a room or an outfit, properly accessorize your tent

Tents typically come with a body, rain fly, poles, stakes, and stuff sack. But there are a few other items you'll need to provide maximum comfort and to prolong the life of your investment.

Most tents come with metal or plastic stakes that are fine for a forest floor or grassy terrain. But for sand or extremely hard ground, there are several different kinds of stakes that will make life much easier. Even if your tent is freestanding, it should still be staked down so it doesn't blow away.

You'll definitely want a ground cloth to protect you and your tent and a tarp to shield rain or to create shade.

Although not a necessity, a freestanding screen room is one of the comforts many campers like to bring along.

Stake It

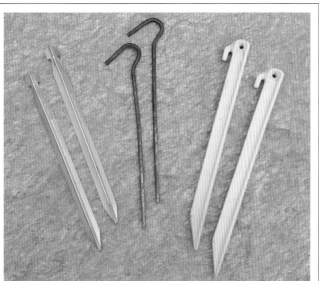

Ground Cloth

Be sure the ground cloth is smaller than the footprint of the tent.

- Traditional metal stakes are shown on the left. For hard-packed or rocky soil, consider small-diameter stakes (pictured in the center).

- A rubber-headed mallet comes in handy for pounding stakes into hard ground.

- Sand stakes (shown on the right) are a must for camping at the beach. They are usually plastic, longer than 10 inches, and have grooves for better grip.

- Tent anchors are sacks filled with sand, snow, rocks, or dirt for situations where tent stakes won't hold, such as soft sand, snow, or rock.

- A ground cloth is advisable for added protection from cold, moisture, sharp rocks, or sticks.

- Purchase a ground cloth made for your tent's size, or cut one yourself from an old tarp.

- It should be a few inches smaller than the footprint of your tent, or else rainwater will get between the two layers.

- If it's too large, simply fold the edges *under* (not *over*, or else rain will form a puddle underneath your tent floor!).

There are many little gizmos you can purchase to make the interior of the tent as cozy as possible, including battery-operated fans, radios, and lights and portable DVD players to watch a movie.

A foldable pocket organizer is handy for personal items like keys, flashlight, and cell phone. There's even one on the market that has built-in speakers for your MP3 player!

Tarps

- A tarp is a versatile piece of gear that can be used in a variety of ways to shield you from rain or sun.

- String a tarp over the tent for added protection in a heavy downpour.

- Set it up over the picnic area to create shade or a dry place to cook and eat.

- Tarps usually have grommeted corners so you can either tie the ends to trees or support it with poles and staked guy lines.

Screen Room

- Set up your picnic table or sitting area inside, safe from stinging bugs.

- Look for a rain gutter system to prevent sagging in the rain.

- Some have removable mesh sides for ventilation if sun protection is the main goal.

- Even if the label says the screen room is flame retardant, do not cook inside it.

SLEEPING BAGS
Choose the right sleeping bag to help ensure a good night's sleep

Down versus synthetic, mummy versus rectangular, single versus double: There are a number of decisions to make in purchasing a sleeping bag. But probably the first factor to consider, as in tent selection, is the kind of climate you'll be camping in most often. Just as tents are rated by season, sleeping bags are rated by temperature.

For instance, if a bag is rated for 32 degrees F, it should keep you warm above freezing. This is typically a summer bag. If you will be doing winter camping, you'll want a bag that is rated below 0 degrees. In between are bags for shoulder season camping (see page 6).

Another factor to consider, however, is how "cold" or "hot" individuals tend to sleep. Women often sleep "colder" than men and if so might want to get a bag that's rated to a lower

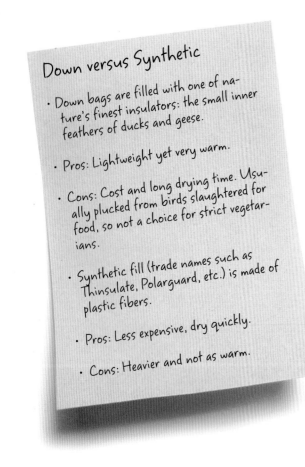

Down versus Synthetic

- Down bags are filled with one of nature's finest insulators: the small inner feathers of ducks and geese.

- Pros: Lightweight yet very warm.

- Cons: Cost and long drying time. Usually plucked from birds slaughtered for food, so not a choice for strict vegetarians.

- Synthetic fill (trade names such as Thinsulate, Polarguard, etc.) is made of plastic fibers.

- Pros: Less expensive, dry quickly.

- Cons: Heavier and not as warm.

Rectangular Bags

- Pros: This shape allows lots of tossing and turning room and is best for children. Youth sizes are available.

- Great for summer camping, they can be opened up completely to be used as a comforter or to sleep on top.

- Very inexpensive styles are available, under $20 in sporting goods departments of major retail stores.

- Cons: Heavy and bulky to roll up, so seldom used by backpackers. Not as warm as mummy bags.

temperature than they expect to be camping in.

Typically, bags with lower temperature ratings are bulkier and heavier, something to consider if you expect to do any backpacking.

The exception to this is the down-filled bag. Down is warmer yet lighter than synthetic bags (see Post-It below for a comparison of materials).

ZOOM

How to pack and store sleeping bags: Inexpensive, rectangular bags can be rolled up and usually come with an attached tie or elastic. Fluffy synthetic or down bags should be gently stuffed into the stuff sack they came with. Store these bags loosely, not stuffed, to preserve their "loft."

Bags should have baffles to keep the material from collecting in one area.

Mummy Bags

- Pros: Mummy bags are the warmest, shaped around the body and cinched around the head to make the most of insulating your body heat.

- They're usually lightweight and stuff compactly, so they're preferred by backpackers.

- Cons: They're more expensive, and you'll probably need to go to an outdoor store or purchase online.

- Restless sleepers or those who like to curl up may find them restrictive. Try to get inside one before committing. Some brands have more room at the hips.

Zip-together Bags

- Get two same-brand rectangular bags and zip them together for couples sleeping.

- Even a mummy bag can be retrofitted to sleep two by purchasing a triangular-shaped coupler that zips to it.

- Some heat will escape at the opening; however, the body heat produced by two people will keep you warmer.

- Bring sheets or sleeping bag liners: They add comfort and keep bags clean longer.

COMFORT
Make your tent a cozy nest with these simple amenities

Sleeping outside doesn't have to mean tossing and turning all night on the cold, hard ground—what we like to call "rotisserie sleeping." Lack of sleep can really sap the enjoyment from the next day's activities, so it's worth putting some thought into your bedding.

Even ultralight backpackers bring along the thinnest of sleeping pads, not only to provide comfort but also to keep the ground from sucking valuable heat from your body. A pad also provides a layer of protection for any moisture that may seep in, as well as protection during a lightning storm.

Foam pads are very inexpensive. If you want a little more comfort yet want to keep bulk down, invest in self-inflating mattresses that still roll up small enough for backpacking.

There are several styles of air mattresses available for camp-

Foam Pads

- Simple sleeping pads are made of either open-cell or closed-cell foam.

- Open-cell foam pads are the least expensive but least comfortable. They feel squishy, so you may feel every rock. They soak up water, so a waterproof covering is necessary.

- Closed-cell foam pads are still inexpensive, but they don't absorb water and are more comfortable. Pitted or egg-crate surfaces trap pockets of warm air.

- Want more cushioning? Use two pads or a folded blanket or comforter.

Self-inflating Mattress

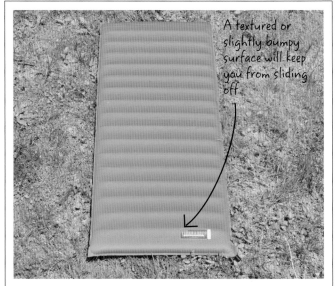

A textured or slightly bumpy surface will keep you from sliding off.

- Basically, open the valve, and the mattresses inflates itself. Blow in a few puffs of air to finish the job.

- Numerous styles are available for backpacking and car camping. Comfort features include pillowtops and fleece coverings.

- They come in different lengths and widths. If space is an issue, consider a three-quarter-length mattress.

- They're not cheap, but investing in a good one will give you years of enjoyment.

ing. If you have room, use the household kind folks buy for overnight guests and snooze in queen-sized comfort.

A sturdy cot is an option for those who have trouble getting up from the ground.

If your mattress comes with a rechargeable pump, be sure it's charged fully before leaving home.

Air Mattress

- Gone are the days of huffing and puffing to inflate a mattress. At the least, a mattress should come with a foot pump.

- Deluxe models have battery-operated or electric pumps attached to them.

- Some pumps operate off a car's cigarette lighter, a good option in case there's no electric outlet in the site.

- Be sure the mattress has a velvety covering on one side. Sleeping on rubber makes your skin feel clammy.

Cots

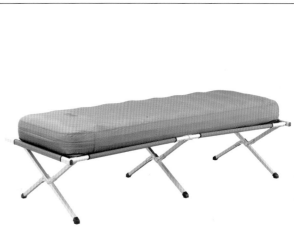

- If the tent is large enough, you can set up cots for really cushy camping.

- A cot is a good option for older people who might have trouble getting up from the ground or for first-time campers afraid of creepy crawlies.

- Be sure the cot's legs are tubular and smooth so they don't tear the tent floor.

- Place an air mattress on top for true luxury.

STOVES

The camping stove is the major purchase and decision in outfitting the camp kitchen

In the old days, camp cooking was almost always done over an open fire. Although a campfire is an enjoyable tradition, it's not the most efficient way to cook: You have to gather wood and wait for a hot bed of coals. There's no temperature control, and the cookware ends up sooty. There are also safety and environmental issues to consider.

Aren't we lucky that today there is a plethora of portable camping stoves to choose from? Some are so simple that all you have to do is turn a knob and light the burner.

There are several types of fuel and many styles and sizes of stoves. First, consider how many burners you'll need: one, two, three, or four. This depends on the number of people

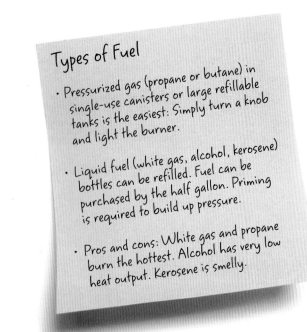

Types of Fuel

- Pressurized gas (propane or butane) in single-use canisters or large refillable tanks is the easiest: Simply turn a knob and light the burner.

- Liquid fuel (white gas, alcohol, kerosene) bottles can be refilled. Fuel can be purchased by the half gallon. Priming is required to build up pressure.

- Pros and cons: White gas and propane burn the hottest. Alcohol has very low heat output. Kerosene is smelly.

Single-burner Stoves

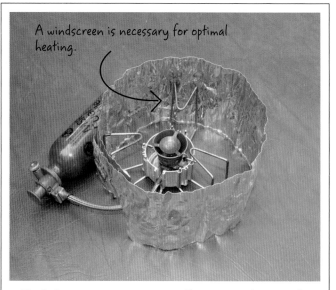

A windscreen is necessary for optimal heating.

- Single-burner stoves serve the minimalist camper's needs just fine. We've used the same white gas stove for over a decade for both backpacking and car camping.

- The simplest kind screws onto a one-time-use canister of propane or butane.

- If you camp a lot, consider a stove that uses refillable liquid fuel bottles. You'll save money and the environment.

- The downside is that liquid fuel stoves require priming and regular cleaning.

you typically camp with but also on how gourmet you like to get outdoors.

Next is the type of fuel. The Post-It below goes into the various options. As with all gear, consider weight and space if you ever plan on backpacking or canoe camping.

Don't forget to bring a lighter or matches in a watertight container or zip-top bag.

Dual-burner Stoves

- The two-burner suitcase-style stove is the workhorse of car camping. The simplest model sets on a picnic table with fold-out windscreen wings.

- The freestanding kind comes with folding legs. Deluxe three- or four-burner models have a meal-prep table and shelves.

- These stoves may come with an attached refillable liquid fuel tank or fittings for a propane tank.

- You'll save money and the environment with a refillable propane tank, the same kind used for backyard gas grills.

Charcoal Grill

- The next-best way to get the taste of campfire cooking is the charcoal grill.

- The portable freestanding grill or hibachi sits on the picnic table or ground.

- Rather than gathering wood, simply buy a bag of charcoal. The pre-treated kind doesn't even require lighter fluid.

- In about fifteen minutes, you'll have a nice bed of coals for grilling meat, vegetables, silver turtles, or shish kebabs, Even marshmallows can be toasted over charcoal.

ESSENTIAL COOKWARE

Gather and organize these very basic items required to cook simply in the outdoors

The reason most people even consider camping is to get outdoors, relax, and commune with nature. The less time one has to spend getting ready, the better.

The key to getting out on a camping trip with minimal stress is to have the basic camp kitchen items organized and packed ahead of time.

Use our lists to create packs or kits for each function. Build on them based on personal preference. Add to or subtract from the lists and the kits after each trip based on what was used or forgotten.

Once at camp, it will be easy to pull out the labeled tubs and zip-top bags as they're needed rather than waste time

Essentials Checklist
- Pots and pans
- Small cutting board
- Large spoon, paring knife, chopping knife, spatula
- Can and bottle opener
- Matches/lighter
- Pot holder, dish towel
- Dish soap and sponge; laundry detergent
- Small trash bags (like those from the grocery store)
- Hand sanitizer
- Add your own items:

Portable Camp Kitchen

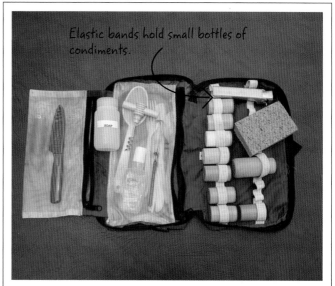

Elastic bands hold small bottles of condiments.

- A portable kitchen, either purchased or homemade, keeps cooking essentials organized and in one place, always ready to go.

- Mesh-covered, zippered compartments can hold utensils, sponge, and soap.

- This basic, portable style is small enough to put into a backpack and take anywhere.

- Larger models are on the market that have room for you to include additional items.

sifting through a hodge-podge of gear in the trunk.

This spread details the most essential kitchen items needed to cook simply in the outdoors. Subsequent pages in this chapter give advice on taking things a step further for the outdoor gourmet, items needed for the tabletop, recipe staples so you won't have to borrow sugar from a neighbor, and items needed for safe food and water storage.

ZOOM

Weight, cost, heating efficiency, and durability are factors in choosing camp cookware: Aluminum: Lightweight, inexpensive, heats quickly, but burns food easily. Stainless steel: Heavier and more durable, cooks more efficiently. Titanium: Durable and the lightest of all options but very expensive. Coveted by backpackers. Cast iron: Cooks evenly and is great for baking. Extremely heavy but lasts forever if taken care of (see page 214 for caring for cast iron).

Camp Condiments

- Always have these basic liquids on hand: cooking oil, olive oil, vinegar, soy sauce, honey, and maple syrup.

- Purchase in small containers to save space. More economical, however, are leakproof, unbreakable plastic bottles that can be refilled as needed. Be sure to label them.

- Include small salt and pepper shakers and cubes of chicken bullion.

- Individual packets of mustard, ketchup, mayonnaise, and salad dressing save space and don't need refrigeration.

Pots and Pans

- Sets of nesting pots like backpackers use save space in the gear box.

- They usually come in three sizes, with foldable handles or a pot gripper if handleless, and slip into a mesh ditty bag. Choose the size of your set based on the number of people.

- They are made of a variety of metals (see Zoom sidebar above for pros and cons).

- Flat lids with sides can be used as a plate or frying pan or flipped over on top of the pot to create a double boiler.

ADDITIONAL COOKING GEAR

The outdoor gourmet will want to add some special items for creating memorable camp meals

The one-pot-meal school of thought is fine for many. But those who want to move their gourmet skills from kitchen to camp will need some additional items.

The gourmet cook requires function-specific utensils and good, sharp knives of varying sizes.

A Dutch oven is a fabulous invention that simulates the all-around cooking of a traditional oven. A Dutch oven is nestled into the hot coals of a fire, with more added on top. An outback oven is an alternative that can be placed on top of a stove.

A large cast-iron griddle makes it possible to cook pancakes or hamburgers all at once rather than feeding folks one at a time.

Additional Gear Checklist
- Colander/strainer
- Griddle, Dutch oven
- Utensils: Slotted spoon, tongs, ladle, vegetable peeler, corkscrew
- Cheese grater
- Tablecloth, napkins
- Kebab-style skewers
- Measuring cups and spoons
- Knife set
- Tub for washing dishes

Dutch Oven

Turn the lid over and use it as a griddle.

- A round, deep-sided pot with a flat fitted lid can bake anything from sticky buns to lasagna.

- Most often made of cast iron, but aluminum models, light enough even for backpacking, are available.

- The pot is nestled into the coals of a wood or charcoal fire. Place hot coals or charcoal briquettes, or build a twiggy fire on the flat lid to simulate baking.

- It can also be used to deep fry, roast, bake, or stew.

Many campsites have charcoal grills, but if not, bring a portable gas or charcoal grill. Portable smoker/grill combos allow the backyard chef to smoke ribs, grill meat, and even deep-fry using propane or charcoal.

Instant or bagged coffee doesn't satisfy most coffee aficionados. A French press or percolator makes terrific camp coffee with ease.

Today you'll find all kinds of gourmet items for camping: from fondue sets to battery-operated ice cream makers.

Additional Utensils

- Plastic or wood utensils protect nonstick cookware from scratching. Lexan is a durable plastic alternative.

- Metal utensils, however, will not be damaged when cooking on an open fire or grill. Don't forget long-handled tongs and spatula for grilling.

- Keep utensils together on a ring or in a mesh ditty bag or zippered pouch.

- Bring good, sharp knives of various sizes. Knife blades should be covered for protection.

Camp Coffee

- An unbreakable French press is an inexpensive way to make delicious fresh coffee.

- A French press coffee mug is good for making one cup at a time.

- An old-fashioned aluminum or enamelware percolator simulates the electric drip coffee maker. It's a good choice if making coffee for a crowd because it comes in all sizes.

- There's even a camp-model drip coffee maker that fits over the stove burner.

TABLETOP

Everything needed to set the table for memorable and relaxing mealtimes

A picnic table set with tablecloth and napkins, a lit lantern in the middle as dusk descends. This is the way to enjoy a good meal cooked in the outdoors.

But that ambience can easily be ruined by last-minute scrounging around for enough forks for everyone.

There are two ways to do it: Get everyone his or her own personal mess kit, or purchase a full-on table setting for the family, all organized in a neat carrying case.

Some parents choose to have children responsible for reassembling their own mess kits at the end of meal clean-up.

Bring a mesh ditty bag to put wet dishes in to air dry.

Some people like to take paper plates camping, but we're

Tabletop Checklist
- Tablecloth and napkins
- Utensils, personal and serving
- Plate, bowl, mug
- Hot pads
- Lantern and/or citronella candles
- Bug spray (they always seem to know when it's dinnertime!)

Double Duty

- Minimalist campers like to keep mealtime simple.

- A shallow bowl can serve as a plate or a bowl. A large mug can be used for hot drinks or soup, eliminating the need for a bowl.

- Sporks—combined forks and spoons—reduce the number of utensils floating around.

- A flat pot lid with tall sides can be flipped over for a serving dish or an extra plate.

not big fans of disposables. If you do have a large group and not enough plates, by all means use paper, not foam, disposables. Instead of tossing them into the garbage to head for a landfill, you can burn them in the fire, and there will be no waste.

Personal Mess Kit

- Mess kits typically contain fork, spoon, knife, bowl, plate, and mug that nest together.

- Items can be made of aluminum, titanium, plastic, or durable Lexan.

- Mess kits should nest together and slip into a ditty bag to keep items together.

- A mesh ditty bag is handy at clean-up time. After washing, simply hang the wet items from a post or tree to air dry.

Table Setting

- The gourmet family might consider purchasing a complete tableware set for two four, six, or eight people

- Plates, bowls, mugs, utensils, even cloth napkins, all have a place.

- They may be made of plastic, Lexan, or the classic blue enamelware that will last a lifetime.

- Tableware sets come in a zippered carrying case, a picnic basket, or a lidded box that doubles as a large bowl and serving tray.

RECIPE STAPLES

Keep one tub of staples resupplied at all times for a complete camping pantry

Dried or canned nonperishables can be kept in your camping pantry for months. Simply keep a list of the perishables, like meat, veggies, milk, and eggs, to get at the last minute.

Keep these nonperishable lists to restock the staple box after each camping trip, and you'll always be ready to head out the door.

The camp gourmet needs a variety of herbs and spices for tasty international and innovative menus. Build your own spice kit, and you'll be ready to follow any recipe.

Even baking outdoors need not be intimidating. Spice up the camp menu with some home-baked goodness. Try practicing at home with a fun family activity for the backyard. A

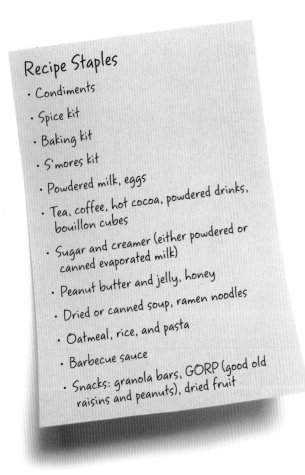

Recipe Staples

- Condiments
- Spice kit
- Baking kit
- S'mores kit
- Powdered milk, eggs
- Tea, coffee, hot cocoa, powdered drinks, bouillon cubes
- Sugar and creamer (either powdered or canned evaporated milk)
- Peanut butter and jelly, honey
- Dried or canned soup, ramen noodles
- Oatmeal, rice, and pasta
- Barbecue sauce
- Snacks: granola bars, GORP (good old raisins and peanuts), dried fruit

Spice Kit

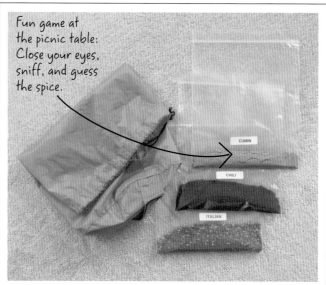

Fun game at the picnic table: Close your eyes, sniff, and guess the spice.

CUMIN
CHILI
ITALIAN

- Fill and label small zip-top baggies with the herbs and spices you use most often. Place the baggies in a larger ditty bag to keep organized.

- Alternative: Buy the smallest herb and spice containers available and place them in a covered plastic box.

- Pack as many or as few seasonings as you typically use at home (see sidebar above on types of herbs and spices).

- For simplicity, purchase a multi-shaker made for camping containing about six of the most popular spices.

32

baking kit is as simple as the four basic ingredients for bread: flour, yeast, salt, and water.

Whether or not you have kids, you'll probably want to have the ingredients for s'mores on every camping trip. Buy a gourmet s'mores kit, or simply purchase the ingredients for the food tub.

ZOOM

The basic seasonings are salt, pepper, and garlic, either powdered or fresh cloves. Build on these depending on the type of cooking you do:
Italian: oregano, basil, parsley, marjoram, bay leaf
Oriental: curry, cumin, powdered mustard, cayenne, wasabi powder
Tex-Mex: chili powder, crushed red pepper
Seafood: tarragon, lemongrass, dill, fennel, thyme, paprika, Old Bay
Grilling: rosemary, prepared rubs
Baking: nutmeg, cinnamon

S'mores are a Girl Scout invention, short for the phrase "some more."

Baking Kit

- Baking outdoors is easy with the basic ingredients on hand and a Dutch or outback oven.

- The simplest way is to purchase all-in-one instant mixes for blueberry muffins, cornbread, or even cheesecake. Just add water or milk.

- Keep stocked the ingredients for quick bread: flour, baking powder, sugar, powdered milk, salt, and oil.

- For variations, stock cornmeal, yeast, vanilla, whole wheat flour, dried fruit, chopped nuts, and canned pie filling.

S'mores Kit

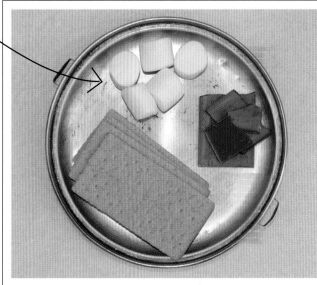

- S'mores—toasted marshmallows and a chocolate bar sandwiched between two graham crackers—are a camping tradition.

- Create your own kit by stocking graham crackers, chocolate bars, marshmallows, and long metal skewers to prevent burned fingers.

- Don't want to build a fire? Gourmet s'mores kits are now on the market that enable you to make them on the tabletop.

- Kits have a wooden platter with compartments for the ingredients, a mini-hibachi grill, and bamboo skewers.

GEAR: KITCHEN

WATER & FOOD STORAGE

Keeping food cold and water clean is tops on the camping safety list

Most likely there will be a potable fresh water supply in your campground, perhaps even in your site. You'll still want to bring some type of container to have water easily accessible in your camp kitchen.

On occasion, such as in primitive state forests or beach campsites, you will need to bring your own fresh water or filter a local water source.

On long hikes where you do not want to carry all your water, bring a water filter or iodine tablets to treat water from a natural source.

Never drink surface water without treating it. Even crystal clear mountain streams can contain girardia, a naturally occurring

Water and Food Storage

- Cooler or mini-fridge
- Personal water bottles
- Large water containers for camp
- Zip-top bags for food
- Water-tight plastic containers for food
- Water purification: tablets or filter

Keeping Food Cold

Drape a wet towel across the cooler: Condensation helps keeps the interior c

- A small, soft-sided cooler is handy for lunches for day trips and can be easily stuffed into a kayak or daypack.

- A large cooler on wheels makes transporting to the campsite or beach much easier.

- If there's electricity in your site, and you don't want to be running to the store for ice, consider a mini-fridge. There will be plenty of room for that case of beer!

- Other coolers run off your car's cigarette lighter; just be sure you don't run down the battery!

parasite that causes diarrhea and vomiting.

The amount of fresh food and cold drinks you like to bring will determine the size of cooler or mini-fridge you purchase. A small, soft-sided cooler may be enough for the minimalist who brings limited fresh food. Be sure to bring an extra cooler if you plan on fishing.

Choose virtually indestructible BPA-free Nalgene bottles over disposable water bottles.

To counter the taste of iodine, add a lemon peel or powdered drink mix to water bottles.

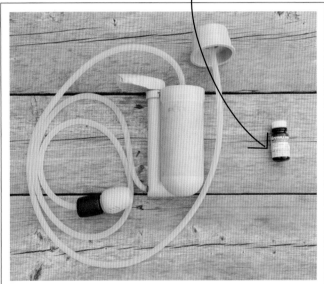

Water Storage

- In the ideal camping world, you have a spigot of potable water right in your campsite. Bring a bucket, jug, or tub for washing dishes.

- Often tent sites do not have their own water spigot, so use a collapsible plastic container or jug to bring water from the nearest faucet.

- Bring individual water bottles to have water in the tent at night and on day hikes.

- Hydration systems like CamelBak make it easy to stay hydrated during physical exertion.

Water Treatments

- Drink only from known, potable water sources. There are three basic treatments for purifying water:

- Bring to a rolling boil for at least five minutes, or dissolve iodine tablets for at least twenty minutes.

- The most effective method is a pump water filter/purifier: The charcoal filter strains out parasites; the purifier contains iodine to kill viruses.

- Now available are individual water bottles with a water filtration system in the cap, so it purifies as you drink.

GENERAL CLOTHING

Plan for all types of weather conditions you're likely to encounter

First check your closet for old or worn clothes you don't mind getting dirty. These will suffice for your general around-camp clothing and general activities. But if you plan on longer hikes, especially in hot weather or high altitudes, you'll want some specific, more technical clothing.

In any weather, take a good rain jacket and preferably rain pants as well.

Hot summer days are notorious for bringing on thunderstorms. Even in summer a hiker can get chilled to the bone, even bordering on hypothermia. If you've ever been wearing a sweat-soaked cotton T-shirt on top of a mountain when a squall comes up, you know the feeling.

Desert climates, common in the southwest U.S., pose a real clothing challenge. In summer, daytime temps well over 100

Convertible pants with legs that zip off to shorts are an ingenious solution.

Basic Clothing for Warm Weather Camping

- Shorts
- T-shirts
- Bathing suit
- Underwear
- Socks
- Sleepwear
- Hat

Hiking Clothes

- For a leisurely walk in the woods, shorts and T-shirt may be fine.

- For more serious hiking, you'll be more comfortable with more specific clothing of lightweight, breathable fabrics.

- Long pants with cuffs that cinch protect from prickly bushes, rocks, poison ivy, and ticks. Shorts keep your leg muscles cool and allow more movement.

- Even if you start in short sleeves, be sure to have a sweater or fleece in your daypack. Shirt sleeves that roll up are nice.

degrees can plummet 50 degrees or more at night.

If you'll be camping in colder weather, invest in a layering system of performance fabrics (see next spread).

Finally, don't forget pajamas or at least a comfortable set of clothes reserved for sleeping. Wearing camp clothes to bed brings dirt, sweat, moisture, and odors into the tent.

(see next spread)

ZOOM

Cotton breathes, allowing perspiration to escape, great on a warm day. Cons: It gets and stays wet, sucking heat from your body on a cold day.

Wool conducts heat poorly, making it an excellent insulator, even when wet. Cons: It's heavy and bulky when wet and dries slowly.

Synthetics insulate yet wick moisture away from the skin. They absorb virtually no water and dry quickly, making them easy to hand wash and hang dry. Cons: They retain odors.

Armpit zippers are wonderful for ventilation.

Hot Weather Clothes

Rain Gear

- You'll be cooler in light-weight clothing of cotton or wicking synthetic that covers your skin rather than leaving skin exposed to the sun.

- Wear loose-fitting, light-colored clothing to reflect sunlight.

- Clothing with Ultraviolet Protection Factor (UPF) built in and laundry additives that add Sun Protection Factor (SPF) to existing clothing are available.

- If swimming is an option, wear quick-dry shorts or a bathing suit under your clothes.

- A rain poncho is okay for short summer hikes but not for longer hikes, shoulder seasons, or summits.

- Invest in a good, brand name jacket and pants of waterproof yet breathable material like polypropylene. You'll never regret it.

- Be sure the jacket has a hood. A bill on the front keeps rain off the face.

- Avoid rain gear that is too bulky because it should go in your daypack. A jacket that self-stuffs into a pocket is nice.

37

LAYERING CLOTHING
Layer clothing for optimum comfort in the outdoors

The principle behind layering is that several light layers are better than one heavy layer. In this spread we'll help you choose three layers made of materials that insulate and allow moisture to escape while keeping it from entering.

On a purely pragmatic level, it's easier to take layers off as you get hot and to put them back on, for example, after you've reached the top of a windy peak.

In a nutshell, you want a polypropylene base layer, a fleece mid-layer, and a waterproof shell outer layer.

Cotton, when wet, pulls heat from the body and dries very slowly, making it a very poor and potentially dangerous choice in cold environments (hence the phrase "cotton kills"). For this reason, we don't recommend cotton in any part of a good layering system.

Under Layer

- Wear a long-sleeved top and long bottoms of synthetic or a synthetic/wool blend, never cotton.

- Forgo your regular underpants completely if they're made of cotton.

- A zip-up collar will keep your neck warm and allow ventilation.

- If chafing is a problem, consider a spandex (Lycra) undergarment. It is sheer, stays put, and produces no rubbing.

Mid-layer

- A fleece or wool sweater and hiking pants are good choices for a mid-layer.

- Choose lightweight wool or micro fleece for warmer climes and bulkier, chunky fleece or a heavy-pile sweater in cold.

- Many prefer a fleece vest to long sleeves. It insulates the core while allowing ventilation for the arms.

- A wind shirt is another nice option for mid-layer. The tightly woven fabric keeps chill winds out and is usually somewhat water resistant in a light rain.

Wool is a good mid-layer for its natural insulating properties, but it dries very slowly and requires laundry care to prevent shrinkage. Virgin wool retains oil from the sheep and dries a bit faster.

Synthetics are the best choice for keeping you warm and dry. They wick moisture away from your skin, dry quickly, and can be made waterproof. Downsides: They hold odors and are petroleum based, so they will melt.

Outer Layer

- In warmer climates, a lightweight rain jacket and pants will do.

- Choose a heavyweight jacket for colder weather, being sure to buy a size large enough to go over the under and mid-layers.

- In either case, the outer layer should be waterproof and windproof and have a cinchable hood.

- In snowy, winter weather, you might want an insulated jacket filled with down or synthetic fill.

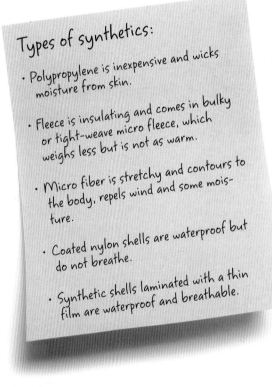

Types of synthetics:

- Polypropylene is inexpensive and wicks moisture from skin.

- Fleece is insulating and comes in bulky or tight-weave micro fleece, which weighs less but is not as warm.

- Micro fiber is stretchy and contours to the body, repels wind and some moisture.

- Coated nylon shells are waterproof but do not breathe.

- Synthetic shells laminated with a thin film are waterproof and breathable.

FOOTWEAR

Happy feet make happy campers, so be sure to research carefully when picking your footwear

Although you don't want to fill up the car with shoes, everyone should have at least two pairs for camping: one for outdoor activities and one for around camp.

Consider the activities you'll be engaging in: climbing mountains, walking rivers, boating, traversing boulder fields, or playing a game of basketball.

If there's one thing to take care of, it's your feet. If they're wet, cold, or blistered, you're not going to be a happy camper.

Hiking shoes provide cushioning from rocks and support for arches and ankles, reducing the possibility of leg cramps or sprains. They can be waterproofed so you can walk even through shallow streams.

Camp Shoes

These Crocs have a heel strap that can be flipped up or down.

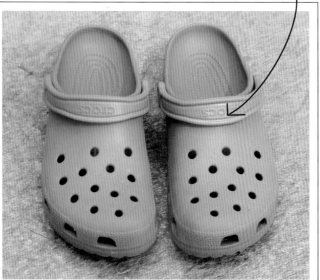

- Shoes for around camp should be comfortable and slip easily on and off.

- Crocs are a great, light-weight option that can also be used in the water or even worn in a public shower.

- Other options are light sneakers, flip-flops, sandals, or the popular hybrid sneaker-sandal that can also be worn for easy trail or river walking.

- In case it gets cold at night, choose a shoe with which a sock can be worn, that is, no toe thong.

Light-duty Hikers

- These are fine for most day-hiking on easy, well-maintained trails. They're not suitable for technical surfaces like boulder fields, steep inclines, and alpine environments or when carrying a heavy backpack.

- Categories include cross-trainer, trekking, trail-running, and trail sandals.

- They're lightweight so you don't get as tired wearing them. Breathable materials and vents keep your feet cool.

- They don't provide ankle support, but many believe this strengthens the ankle.

If canoeing or kayaking, you'll want to wear a shoe or sandal that can get wet.

After a day of hiking or boating or whatever, get those wet or muddy shoes off and into something comfortable.

At the end of the day you'll want to slip on a loose, comfortable camp shoe for sitting around the fire and slipping off to pop into the tent.

ZOOM

Get hiking shoes that fit. Visit a reputable outdoor store with a large selection and trained sales assistants. Ask for a fitting. In an unlaced boot, slide your foot forward so the toes touch the front. There should be a finger's width of space behind the heel. Lace them up and walk around. Look for an incline to simulate trekking uphill and down.

High-tech wool blends are warm, cushioned at the heel, moisture wicking, and quick drying.

Heavy-duty Hikers

- When **carrying** heavy packs or hiking **on** rough, technical terrain, consider heavy-duty boots with good ankle and arch support.

- High leather uppers encircle the ankle, protecting from sprains. Hard soles protect from rocks.

- Leather/fabric combinations allow for more breathability but are not generally as waterproof. For completely waterproof and/or cold-weather boots, consider all-leather or a product like GORE-TEX.

- Be sure to buy waterproofing treatment t.

Socks

- Socks provide warmth and moisture wicking and prevent blisters.

- Cotton is fine for around camp and light activities, but when wet from perspiration it causes friction, which can lead to blisters. As with clothing, synthetic or wool is better.

- Wear thicker socks with larger boots and in cold weather; wear thinner socks for light-duty boots and in warm weather.

- Wear high socks to protect from scratches and ticks.

GEAR: PERSONAL

HEAD & HANDS
Hats and gloves protect from sun, rain, cold, and insects

Consider the chilly autumn or spring morning. You'd like to build a fire, but your hands are numb! Too bad you forgot gloves.

The head and the hands are the body parts most often left exposed and through which we lose a lot of body heat. If warmth and comfort are your priorities, then a baseball or vented cap is not the way to go.

Fashion versus function: Choose a hat that will insulate or provide sun protection rather than one that just looks good. Avoid stiff-brimmed or straw hats that can be crushed. Opt for foldable or stuffable styles.

For warmth, nothing beats a close-fitting wool cap. It's small, lightweight, and easy to throw into your pack. If you're still cold, put on your rain jacket and cinch the hood. It will

Warm Hat

- A warm wool or synthetic fleece hat is one of the easiest and best ways to regulate your body temperature.

- It's true that you lose a tremendous amount of heat from the head.

- A close-fitting skull cap will keep you warm when you sleep or summit a peak.

- Caps are small and lightweight, so it's easy to keep one in the tent and an extra in the daypack.

Sunhat

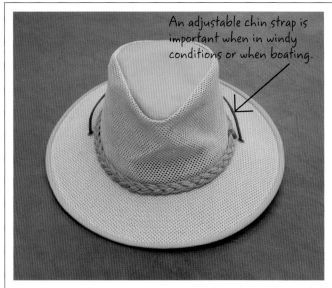

An adjustable chin strap is important when in windy conditions or when boating.

- Ball caps protect only your forehead, eyes, and upper cheeks, leaving your neck and ears, common places for skin cancer, completely exposed.

- A wide-brimmed hat will not only protect you from the sun but also keep you cooler.

- Look for a foldable or stuffable hat rather than straw, which will get crushed.

- Quick-drying and water-resistant fabrics are nice for water sports and rain.

also keep cold air from going down your back.

So don't bury that winter gear come camping season. Warm hats and gloves have a place in your colder-season camping. Remember that you'll be outside, not in your warm house.

There should be a Velcroed or zippered opening to allow eating and drinking.

Bug Hoods

- Unfortunately, mosquitoes and no-see-ums are a fact of life for campers.

- If you're going to a place that's notorious for them, consider a bug hood or shirt to don at dusk, when they are most likely to swarm.

- Bug shirts protect your entire upper torso with a combination of mesh and solid fabric. Long sleeves cinch at the cuff to keep bugs off the arms.

- In hot weather, a bug hood and lots of insect repellant may be a better choice.

Gloves and Mittens

- Gloves allow for more dexterity for doing camp chores. Mittens are better for warmth because fingers heat each other.

- Choose lightweight, medium, or winter gloves, depending on the season.

- Synthetic gloves are good for wind and water protection, but beware melting them while cooking or tending the fire. Wool is very warm and won't melt, but if it gets wet, it dries very slowly.

- If planning to summit a peak, throw a pair into your daypack for the top.

GEAR: PERSONAL

43

HYGIENE

Give some thought to personal hygiene products for maximum comfort

A camping friend once said: "Just because we're *in* the woods doesn't mean we have to look like we're *from* the woods." We would add *smell* to that statement!

Tents are close quarters, so for your comfort and that of others, camping isn't the time to let personal hygiene slide.

Don't bring full-sized versions of everything in your bath-

room. Fill smaller bottles with shampoo, bath gel, and other liquids. Head to the travel- or trial-size section of your local pharmacy.

Keep shower items in a ditty bag to take to the bathhouse, and wear a pair of waterproof shoes, like Crocs or flip-flops.

Do some preventive maintenance just before you leave

Toiletries

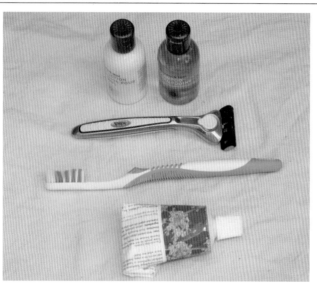

- A fold-out toiletry bag is convenient for taking to the bathhouse.

- Buy trial sizes or fill small containers with soap, hand sanitizer, shampoo, conditioner, toothpaste, deodorant, powder, and lotion.

- Don't forget toothbrush, floss, lip balm, comb/brush, razor, feminine products, cotton swabs, a small sewing kit, and bar soap in a case.

- Baby wipes and facial cleansing wipes are indispensable when you can't get to water.

Bathroom Items

- Even if the campground has bathrooms, it never hurts to have a roll of toilet paper in case they run out.

- A partial roll of toilet paper is easier to pack than a full one.

- Personal wipes and hand sanitizer are a good idea for the bathroom kit.

- If you'll be going hiking, be sure to bring these items, along with a backpacker's trowel in case nature calls unexpectedly and you have to dig a cathole.

home: pluck eyebrows, shave legs, and trim nails (they'll just get dirt under them anyway!).

Forgo makeup or a high-maintenance hairstyle for a ponytail, headband, baseball cap, or bandanna. You may not have electricity for that hair dryer or curling iron.

The bottom line is you don't really need to shower every single day. Take a few days off and save some water.

Towels made especially for backpackers are extremely light and quick drying.

Towels

- Don't forget to bring bath towels and beach towels for everyone in the family.

- Assign everyone a different color to avoid sharing towels and spreading germs.

- Look in the linen closet for your old, worn, or stained towels.

- However, terrycloth towels are bulky and take forever to dry. Consider quick-drying micro-fiber travel towels that are highly absorbent and compact.

Solar Shower

- Not all campgrounds have showers. If you can't go without one, consider a solar shower.

- The simple device consists of a heavy-duty PVC pouch, a flexible hose, and an on-off switch.

- Simply hang the shower in the sun to heat about five gallons of water in a few hours.

- The water can also be used for washing dishes.

GEAR: PERSONAL

PERSONAL NECESSITIES
Create your own necessity bag for things you want handy at all times

There are probably certain personal items that you'd like to keep with you at all times, whether camping, hiking, or kayaking—or doing most anything outdoors!

They can go into a simple ditty bag, a small duffel bag, daypack, or small dry bag in the case of kayaking.

Everyone in camp should have a small flashlight or headlamp for getting up to go to the bathroom in the middle of the night, finding things in the tent, or reading. When packing, reverse or remove the batteries to prevent the flashlight from being turned on accidentally and draining the batteries.

Each adult will likely want a Swiss Army Knife or multi-purpose tool like a Leatherman.

Keep a Necessity Bag Handy and Take It into the Tent at Night
- Flashlight and extra batteries
- Water bottle
- Toilet paper or tissues
- Knife
- Bug spray, sunscreen
- Important medications
- Sunglasses, reading glasses
- Book or notebook
- Small first aid kit
- Watch
- Rain jacket

Personal Lighting

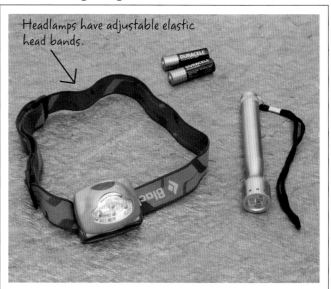

Headlamps have adjustable elastic head bands.

- The beauty of a headlamp is that it is hands free so you can prepare a meal, set up a tent, or read in the dark.

- Even children can have their own small penlight or a key chain fob that stays on only when the button is depressed.

- Don't forget spare batteries, preferably the rechargeable kind. Chargers can be solar powered or plug into a car's cigarette lighter.

- A larger lantern-style or torch light is good for general camp lighting.

Parents will likely add their own items to the mix: an extra pacifier or a favorite toy.

A good daypack will make a walk in the woods much more enjoyable. Get one big enough so that you'll be prepared for cold, rain, sun, hunger, or emergencies but not so big that you'll be tempted to fill it to an unwieldy weight.

Daypack

- Look for a contoured, padded back panel and comfortable, adjustable shoulder straps.

- A waist belt keeps the weight off shoulders and on the hips. Sternum straps distribute weight across the chest.

- Look for side pockets to carry water bottles and/or an interior pouch to accommodate a hydration bladder like CamelBak.

- A large top pocket provides easy access to maps or anything you want to grab quickly: sunscreen, lip balm, snacks, or tissues.

Personal Knife

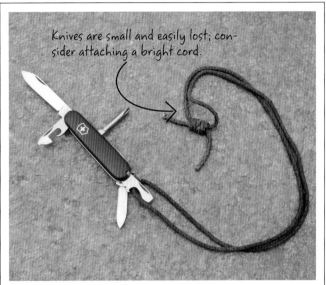

Knives are small and easily lost; consider attaching a bright cord.

- A good knife is invaluable for cutting food or rope, opening food packages, or making wood shavings for a fire.

- Knives should be sharp and have a locking blade to prevent closing on fingers accidentally.

- The most basic ones usually have two sizes of blades, screwdrivers (flat and Phillips), and bottle and can openers.

- Deluxe models may have scissors, pliers, corkscrew, tweezers, small saw, fish scaler, ruler, wire cutter, or nail file.

GEAR: PERSONAL

BREAKFAST

Plan the most important meal of the day to provide energy for camping

If you have the time, it's fun to make a big, hot breakfast before a day of outdoor activity. If you'd rather get an early start for hiking or boating, go with a quick breakfast, and bring some mid-morning snacks.

For kids, camping might not be the time to try something new. Think about comfort foods they eat at home, and try to replicate them in camp so they truly feel "at home" in the outdoors.

Bring their favorite cereal. Bake granola or your special zucchini bread at home and bring it along. If you have a food dehydrator, dry some favorite fruits for healthy snacks.

For many families, the big Sunday breakfast is a tradition

Quick Breakfast

Purchase liquid eggs in a carton to freeze for easy transport.

- Cold cereal, individual yogurts, granola bars, fresh fruit or fruit cups, bagels, and peanut butter require no cooking.

- Just add boiling water to individual packets of instant oatmeal, grits, or cream of wheat.

- Hard-boil eggs at home, then peel and eat cold for breakfast.

- Bring store-bought coffee cake or doughnuts and serve with fruit.

Comfort Breakfast

- The classic fried eggs, bacon, and hash browns taste even better in an iron skillet over a fire or camp stove.

- Make a big pot of oatmeal, grits, or cream of wheat, and put out an array of additions to choose from: raisins, dried cranberries, brown sugar, nuts.

- Make French toast the same way as at home: Dip bread in a mixture of egg, milk, and cinnamon and fry in a pan.

- Make coffee cake, sticky buns, or scones in a Dutch oven.

that is easily transferable to camp. Fried eggs, sizzling bacon, and hash browns are staples, tasting even better over a fire and cooked in a cast-iron skillet.

Don't forget to factor clean-up time into the morning routine. Dishes must be washed and put away (just like home!) and trash disposed of after every meal to prevent attracting animals.

Breakfast Gourmet

A side of sausage links, the pre-cooked kind for quick cooking.

Easy Orange Muffins

- Cut an orange in half and take out the insides.

- Put prepared instant muffin mix in one half.

- Replace other half and wrap in foil.

- Place in the hot coals of a fire to bake for fifteen to twenty minutes.

- Recipe courtesy of Old 96 District South Carolina.

- Bill loves to make blueberry pancakes in camp, smothered in butter and maple syrup.

- Gourmet variation: chocolate banana pecan pancakes. Add powdered hot chocolate and sliced bananas to standard pancake mix, and sprinkle with pecans and chocolate bits.

- Breakfast burritos: a flour tortilla filled with scrambled eggs, chunks of ham, grated cheddar, onions, and peppers and topped with salsa.

- Omelets filled with diced ham, cheese, peppers, onions, and leftover veggies.

LUNCH & SNACKS
Pack scrumptious, nutritious fuel for outdoor activities

Active days on the trail, in the playground, or on the water may require more calories than you're used to needing at home.

At the first pang of hunger or when little ones' feet begin to drag on the trail, reach for a quick snack or stop for an early lunch.

Be sure these aren't empty calories and beware of too much sugar, which gives a false boost of energy. Choose high protein and whole grain carbs for energy foods.

To maximize time out on the trail, multi-task and make sandwiches while prepping breakfast. This means you have to take the food tubs out only once.

Place sandwiches and drinks in a small, soft-sided cooler. Or wrap sandwiches in bandannas to avoid squishing them

Quick Lunch

- For easy eating on the trail, slice cheese and pepperoni for crackers ahead of time.

- Pack canned herring, sardines, or sausages you can eat right out of the can.

- Cut up veggies before hand, whip up a dressing, and put into a compartmented container.

- When in doubt, get take-out! Pick up ready-made sandwiches at a nearby deli or grocery.

Comfort Food

Wraps and pitas travel better than sandwich bre.

- Wraps, pitas, and ciabattas are variations on the tried-and-true lunch sandwich.

- Think protein: peanut butter, tuna fish, chicken, lunch meat and cheese, hummus.

- Then add variations to spice things up. Layer a tortilla wrap with hummus, sliced cucumber, and alfalfa sprouts.

- Tuna, salmon, and chicken now come in easy-open pouches: easier and less messy than opening and draining cans.

in the daypack. If you use containers, be sure they are leak-proof.

Don't forget salt and pepper and condiments like mayonnaise or mustard packets. Bring a small plastic bag for trash.

If you're going to have an in-camp day, might as well make a hot lunch: Open a can of soup, or go all out with a full-course meal.

Flour tortillas can double for burritos or sandwich wraps.

Gourmet Lunch

- Burritos: Layer on a tortilla browned ground beef, chorizo, chicken, refried beans, shredded cheese, lettuce, and tomatoes.

- Pizza in the Dutch oven: pita top with pepperoni, shredded cheese, olives, feta cheese, and spinach.

- Slice a ciabatta lengthwise, toast open faced, layer with cheese, meat, and roasted red pepper or eggplant, fresh rosemary, and olive oil.

- Simple gourmet: imported cheese, a jar of pate or tapenade, smoked salmon, crusty bread, sliced green apple, and wine.

Author's Favorite Wrap

- Spread out on a spinach tortilla:

- Chicken pieces

- Sliced avocado

- Alfalfa sprouts

- Sliced tomato

- Red onion slivers

- Top with ranch dressing, and roll it all up.

MENU PLANNING

51

DINNER

Whether it's simple or gourmet, there's no reason to go to bed hungry

Even minimalist cooks can make great-tasting one-pot meals that require no fuss and leave easy clean-up.

Outdoor gourmets will most likely want to create outdoor versions of their house specialties. Just about all the cooking techniques—grilling, frying, sauteing, boiling, steaming, roasting, broiling, or baking—can be accomplished in the outdoors.

On Burnham family backpacking trips, we rotate meals, with each couple trying to outdo the other for backcountry gourmand. We will never forget when our friend Dwayne roasted a whole chicken on the fire, whipped up instant mashed potatoes, gravy, stuffing, and steamed asparagus in the Great Smoky Mountains. And we were backpacking, no less!

Buying and Packing Smart

- Choose foods that cook quickly to save fuel. Quick brown rice, for instance, takes five minutes compared with forty-five minutes for the regular kind.

- Freeze things like meat or homemade soup to last longer. Plus, they'll keep other items in the cooler cold as they defrost.

- Look for cured meats like kielbasa or chorizo in a vacuum-sealed wrap that don't require refrigeration.

Quick Dinners

Meals using all canned or dry ingredients are best for the last night's meal.

- Pre-packaged, one-pot meals with pasta or rice bases simply require water and possibly oil or milk.

- Red rice and beans and macaroni and cheese are staples at home and at camp.

- Jazz them up with chopped ham, canned shrimp, tuna, chicken or kielbasa, chorizo, or ground beef.

- Add fresh, frozen, or canned veggies like tomatoes, spinach, or broccoli for color.

A word to the wise, forgo bringing pre-cooked spaghetti to save time and water. It adds at least ten pounds to your pack! Some shortcuts don't always work out. Through trial and error, we've found plenty that do and collected some great camp recipes.

With just a little forethought and planning, outdoor dinners can become long-lasting memories.

To save time at camp, pre-chop onions, peppers, or carrots at home.

Comfort Dinners

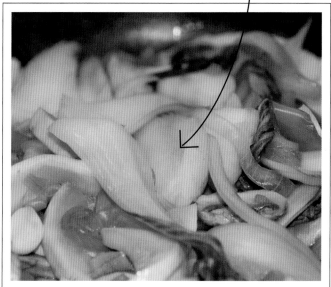

- For a first-night meal, use fresh vegetables and meat.

- Make a stir-fry using fresh veggies like broccoli, bok choy, and sprouts, with either sautéed chicken or tofu over rice.

- Make a tabouleh salad using the quick-cook, pre-seasoned kind, then add fresh tomatoes, parsley, chopped cucumbers, green onions, and lemon juice.

- Root soup: Saute onions, celery, and garlic in olive oil. Add water and diced root vegetables like potatoes, squash, parsnips, or turnips, and simmer until tender.

Gourmet Dinners

- This camp versio of pasta puttanesca uses all nonperishables:

- Sauté in olive oil: garlic, olives, anchovies, canned tomatoes, capers, pine nuts, dried basil, oregano, and parsley. Serve over angel hair pasta and top with grated parmesan.

- Add to pasta primavera: broccoli flowerets, cherry tomatoes, fresh spinach, and chopped ham.

- A low country boil is a one-pot crowd pleaser. Steam in a large kettle: potatoes, ears of corn, sausage, shrimp, whole crabs, and Old Bay seasoning.

MENU PLANNING

CAMPFIRE MEALS
There's a great sense of satisfaction from cooking over a fire

Here's one for the campfire: One of Bill's favorite childhood memories is waking up in the camp to the smell of wood smoke and bacon. Looking out, he could see his dad in his red plaid shirt and blue watch cap cooking over the open flame of the camp fire, putting together a breakfast that would stir Bill's senses and remain strong in his memory over the years.

These days campfires aren't always possible or advised. Even though you should use your stove most often for cooking, try making at least one or two meals over an open fire or a grill. It can be a fun, group activity.

Whether it's wood or charcoal, you don't really cook over a roaring flame. You let it burn down to a glowing bed of hot coals. This, in addition to building the fire, can take some time

Fun Things to Make over a Fire or Grill

- Shish kebabs
- Silver turtles
- Bratwurst
- S'mores
- Dutch oven baking

Quick Campfire Meals

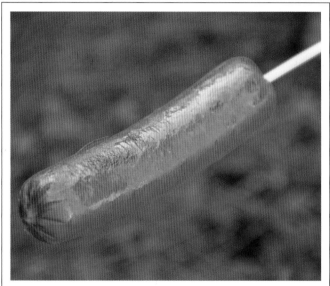

- The kids can make this one: Heat pre-cooked hot dogs on a skewer, then slip them into a bun and top with condiments.

- Place a griddle or freestanding grill over the fire and cook up some pre-made burgers, pre-marinated steaks, or chicken breasts.

- Shish kebabs: Chop red and green peppers, use whole cherry tomatoes, pearl onions, and mushrooms.

- Alternate on skewer with shrimp or 1-inch chunks of beef, chicken, pineapple, or firm tofu. Cook in fire for fifteen to twenty minutes.

54

and patience, so start well before meal-time.

A Dutch oven requires a fire of wood or charcoal and long cooking time, but it enables you to make things most people can't imagine making outdoors: lasagna, sticky buns, sausage cornbread, even a double-layer chocolate cake. Just don't forget skewers and aluminum foil!

Fold foil securely so juices don't run out.

Comfort Foods in Foil

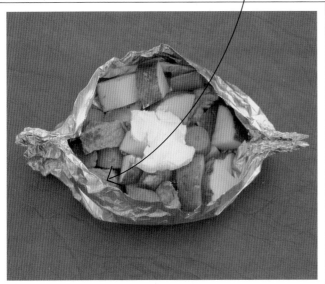

Gourmet Lasagna

- Silver turtles: On a piece of foil place a hamburger patty, potatoes, carrots, onions, salt, pepper, and a dollop of butter.

- Fold foil around turtle, and cook in the coals for twenty minutes.

- Wrap corn on the cob in foil; put on the grill or in the coals of a fire. Do the same for baked potatoes.

- If you get lucky with the fishing pole, wrap the fillets in foil with halved cherry tomatoes, half a lemon, and pinch of garlic salt. Seal and place in coals ten to fifteen minutes.

- Pour a thin layer of seasoned spaghetti sauce into the bottom of a Dutch oven and add a little water.

- Cover with a layer of lasagna noodles. Spread a layer of ricotta or cottage cheese and chopped spinach, then a layer of sauce and a layer of noodles. Repeat until you run out.

- Cover top layer of noodles with sauce, mozzarella, and parmesan cheese. Cover with lid and bake thirty minutes.

- Optional: Add pepperoni or ground beef to the layers.

MENU PLANNING

BEVERAGES
Fluids keep you hydrated and warm you from the inside

Water is without a doubt the best fluid. But let's face it: Sipping warm water all day gets kind of boring.

In hot weather or during physical exertion, it's important for children, especially, to stay hydrated. So have plenty of tasty cold drinks accessible, but avoid too much sugar or caffeine.

New brands of energy water have no calories but add nutrients. Look carefully at the ingredients for added sugar or high-fructose corn syrup. The hotter the weather, the more detrimental are diuretics like coffee, sugary sports drinks, and alcohol.

However, many of us need to jumpstart the day with a good cup of coffee or tea. Hot beverages can also be a safety item: If someone is verging on hypothermia, a hot drink will warm him or her from the inside. Instant chicken bouillon is

Cold Drinks

- In hot weather, have a cooler full of favorite individual juices, iced tea, soda, and water to encourage hydration.

- Water bottles and drinks in pouches can be frozen to provide a refreshing treat and to help keep food cold.

- Box or pouch drinks reduce the amount of trash, but bottles and cans are recyclable.

- Try to limit the number of times the cooler is open for browsing.

Powdered Drinks

- Adding powdered drink mixes to water bottles will make water more palatable to youngsters.

- Lemonade, sports drinks, and iced tea all come in powdered form in packets or jars.

- Try no-carb and no-sugar hydration tablets in your water bottle to optimize electrolyte levels during exercise.

- Powdered drink products produce the least amount of waste because you add them to a cup or water bottle.

a soothing beverage for an upset stomach.

Bring a Thermos of hot tea or other beverage on cold day hikes.

We like to toast the end of a successful day in the outdoors with friends and family with a cup of wine. You might prefer beer or a mixed drink. Be sure to check the campground regulations before bringing it, however. Some state parks do not allow alcohol.

You can take the bladder of wine out of the cardboard box to save space in the cooler.

Comfort Beverages

- Start or end the day with hot tea, cocoa, or coffee.

- Keep a good stock of a variety of tea and chai bags, coffee bags, hot chocolate packets, and chicken bouillon cubes.

- For quick coffee without the instant coffee flavor, place ground coffee into a tea ball and steep in boiling water for several minutes.

- If heading out on a cold or rainy day, put some extra into a Thermos to warm you up throughout the day.

Cocktails

- Boxed wine is perfect for outdoor adventures, and the quality has really improved in recent years.

- Make a batch of Sangria, white, or red wine with fruit like grapes, orange, and lemon slices floating in it.

- Buy pre-mixed cocktail mixes to go with your favorite liquor. Or go gourmet with a hand-cranked blender for margaritas or daiquiris.

- Warm up a cool night around the fire with an Irish coffee or hot toddy.

MENU PLANNING

DESSERTS
Don't forget a sweet treat for around the fire

When planning three meals a day, thinking about dessert may be the last thing on your mind. But dessert can be a fun and exciting part of the camping experience.

Be sure to throw some bags of cookies, snack bars, instant brownie mix, and fresh and canned fruit into the food tub. Keep staples like condensed milk, brown sugar, raisins, and cinnamon for impromptu desserts when the sweet tooth bites.

Tasty desserts can be made on a stick over the fire or in a pot or skillet or baked in a Dutch oven. Some desserts require no cooking at all: See our no-bake cookies below. For a healthy last-night dessert use up all the leftover fruit in a fruit salad. Toss with flaked coconut.

With a little creativity, the options are endless.

The only caveat is to beware of too much sugar at bedtime.

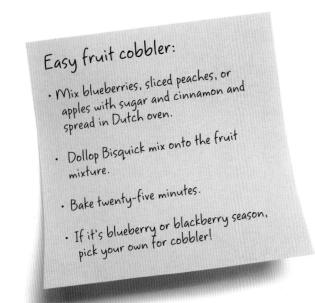

Easy fruit cobbler:

- Mix blueberries, sliced peaches, or apples with sugar and cinnamon and spread in Dutch oven.

- Dollop Bisquick mix onto the fruit mixture.

- Bake twenty-five minutes.

- If it's blueberry or blackberry season, pick your own for cobbler!

Quick Desserts

- Pack some bags of the family's favorites cookies: Fig Newtons, Oreos, chocolate chips. Better yet, make them at home and bring as a homemade surprise.

- Fresh fruit and yogurt, sprinkled with nutmeg or lemon zest, make a super-healthy dessert.

- No-bake cookies: Boil ½ Tbsp dry milk, 1 Tbsp water, 1 Tbsp butter, and ¼ c sugar until it foams. Remove from heat. Add ⅛ tsp vanilla, ⅓ coats, and ¾ Tbsp cocoa powder, stirring after each.

- Drop by spoonfuls onto plates and let set.

For the little ones, falling asleep in a tent can be exciting enough.

Comfort Desserts

- Instant pudding is easy to make in a camp.

- Make an easy custard with milk, egg yolks, sugar, and cornstarch and pour over fresh berries and sponge cake for a quick trifle.

- Stir-fry brownies: Make brownie mix according to directions. Pour a spoonful of oil into a skillet. Cook the batter like scrambled eggs.

- Rice Krispie treats: melt ½ tablespoon butter in a pot. Stir in five marshmallows. When melted, remove from heat and stir in 1 cup Rice Krispies.

Campfire Desserts
- Baked apples: Halve an apple, hollow out the core, and fill with brown sugar and a pat of butter. Wrap in tin foil and place in the coals.

- Banana Boats: Peel one banana and slit open. Stuff with mini-marshmallows and chocolate bits. Wrap in foil and place in fire for five to ten minutes.

- S'mores, of course! Sandwich toasted marshmallows and a chocolate bar between graham crackers.

MENU PLANNING

PACKING: CLOTHING

It's all about organization, so keep in mind these basic principles when planning your wardrobe

Some people are organized, some are not. It's just that simple. But either way, there are some basic principles to keep in mind to avoid that dreaded cry from the tent: "I can't find my [fill in the blank]!"

Be sure that everything has a place and that when you're done using it, it goes back into its place so you know where

it is. This goes for clothing, kitchen gear, and camping gear. It will be an important principle to follow, especially with an extended family camping together.

Have a daypack for things you need to grab quickly or on a regular basis, such as rain gear.

Of course, the season, weather, and activities will dictate

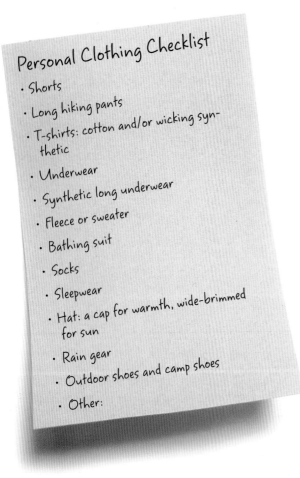

Personal Clothing Checklist

- Shorts
- Long hiking pants
- T-shirts: cotton and/or wicking synthetic
- Underwear
- Synthetic long underwear
- Fleece or sweater
- Bathing suit
- Socks
- Sleepwear
- Hat: a cap for warmth, wide-brimmed for sun
- Rain gear
- Outdoor shoes and camp shoes
- Other:

Clothing Bags

Soft bags make great pillows!

- Over a certain age, each member of the family should have his or her own clothing bag and be responsible for packing and carrying it.

- Label each with a marker, or use bags of different colors. Material should be water resistant in case of rain or

- setting on wet ground.

- Soft duffels are easier to pack and handle than hard-sided suitcases.

- For large families, provide all children with their own laundry bag for their clothes with their name printed on the bag.

types of clothing you bring. Don't take more than you need. A bulky fleece isn't necessary in summer and takes up a lot of room.

Organize clothes by sleeping, dry, and wet clothes. Wet clothes for swimming or boating activities should be quick drying. And you should have plenty of dry socks in your pack.

It's important to do the organizing at home, well before you even start packing. Take stock and do laundry and mending several days before so everything is clean, dried, and folded.

Ditty Bags

- To avoid duffel bag explosion in the tent, have several smaller ditty bags to organize clothing by function inside the larger duffel.

- Have sleeping clothes in a ditty near the top so you can grab them quickly and head into the tent at bedtime.

- Keep socks and underwear in a ditty to keep from getting lost and rain gear in a ditty so they're easily accessible.

- Ditties can be mesh or zip-top bags so you can see what's in them.

Organizing Shoes

- Keep everyone's sneakers, boots, and sandals together to avoid errant shoes from floating around in the car or campground.

- Use a labeled tub, duffel bag, or see-through milk crate.

- You might want to have a clean box and a wet/dirty box so muddy hiking boots don't soil camp shoes and sandals.

- The tent vestibule is a place to kick off your shoes so you don't bring dirt into the tent. Families may want to keep a box here to gather them.

PACKING: GEAR
Achieve a grab-and-go philosophy to get out the door quicker

A grab-and-go style of camping expeditions means getting out the door isn't a hassle each and every time. The goal is to get outdoors more often. This starts with the way you pack.

To pack, start by spreading all your gear out, organized by function, and determining what size containers you'll need for each.

A guide friend who takes large groups out for weeks at a time introduced us to the concept of the action packer, labeled tubs for different functions.

Think about the tasks that need to performed as soon as you get to camp: setting up the kitchen, the tent, the rest of the gear.

Put all the things for setting up the tent in one tub: sleeping pads, tent, poles, drop cloth, stakes, and tarp.

Compression Sacks

- If space is at a premium, look into compression sacks that cinch soft gear down to half its size.

- These sacks are also good for other outdoor activities, such as kayak camping, because they allow for gear to be stuffed into small hatches, but they're excellent for car camping as well.

- Compression sacks cost more but save a lot of space.

- Even regular stuff sacks will cinch items down and keep them from spreading around the car.

Stuffing a Sleeping Bag

- A sleeping bag should be stuffed, not rolled.

- Start at a corner and stuff it far down into the bag.

- Start grabbing by handfuls and stuff all the way to the bottom.

- Pack very tightly at bottom to avoid air pockets. The first three or four stuffs are critical. Cinch the drawing-string tight.

All the things for setting up the kitchen go in another: cookware, tableware, stove, lantern, and flashlight.

All recreational items can go in a third.

The key to being an organized packer is to start with a checklist, revise it after each trip, and keep it in a safe place to pull out again for the next trip.

Use smaller tubs to hold loose items inside the large tubs.

Buy heavy-duty bags; they're not watertight if they break.

Gear Tubs

- Get at least two large plastic tubs; label one "camping gear" and one "kitchen gear."

- The camping tub will hold everything needed to set up the tent: drop cloth, tent, sleeping pads, extra rope, a hammer or mallet for pounding stakes.

- The second tub should hold everything to set up the camp kitchen: cookware, kitchen kit, tableware, lantern, flashlight, water containers, stove if it's small, and fuel.

- A smaller tub could hold tools and repair kits.

Zip-top Bags

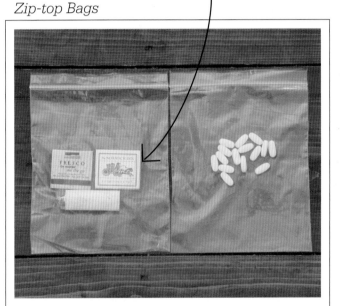

- Use zip-top bags to keep dry items such as matches, toilet paper, or medications.

- Anything spillable—dish soap, laundry soap, hand sanitizer, lotion, fuel—can benefit by being in a zip-top bag to prevent it from spilling on gear.

- Smaller bags, of plastic or mesh, help keep smaller, similar items organized and easy to grab in a hurry.

- Slip playing cards, the book you're reading, or a journal into a gallon-sized zip-top bag to keep it dry.

NONPERISHABLE FOOD
Organized food tubs save time and prevent growling tummies at mealtime

Before camping, first do grocery shopping with a list based on your pre-trip menu planning.

At home, spread your food out and arrange it by meals to be sure you have everything for each day.

Look for ways to reduce packaging by taking bags out of boxes or measuring out only what you will need.

Determine what size tub or tubs you'll need. For just two people, one small tub may do it. A large family or group going out for a week may want to have three food tubs labeled "breakfast," "lunch," and "dinner." This way you need to pull out only the necessary tub from the vehicle.

You may want to group items for each meal together and

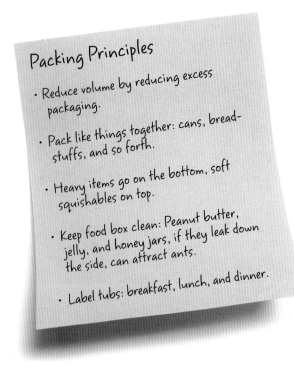

Packing Principles

- Reduce volume by reducing excess packaging.

- Pack like things together: cans, bread-stuffs, and so forth.

- Heavy items go on the bottom, soft squishables on top.

- Keep food box clean: Peanut butter, jelly, and honey jars, if they leak down the side, can attract ants.

- Label tubs: breakfast, lunch, and dinner.

Dry Goods

- Get various sizes of heavy-duty zip-top bags, from snack size to two-gallon.

- To save time at camp, pre-measure items like rice and pancake mix and slip in a note on how much water to add.

- Group like items together, that is, beverages like coffee and tea bags and powdered drinks.

- To keep dirty fingers out of bags of granola, bring some large spoons or measuring cups for serving.

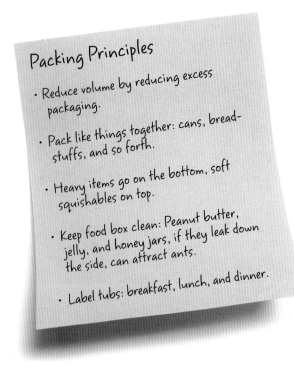

KNACK CAR CAMPING FOR EVERYONE

place them inside a plastic grocery sack or large zip-top bag. This will make mealtime smooth and organized.

Place these smaller bags, cans, and staples into the food tubs, and you're ready to go.

bel bags or containers of items at look alike: sugar, flour, salt.

Remove inner sealed bags from cardboard boxes.

Reduce Packaging

- Repacking camp food causes less bulk, less weight, and less waste.

- Bring only what you need, not the entire five-pound bag of rice or potatoes.

- For baking mixes, pancakes, rice, pasta, oatmeal, and packaged meals, cut out the instructions from the box and slip it inside or tape it to the inner bag.

- Bring twist ties or bag clips to close bags after they are opened.

The Food Tub

- Purchase a durable lidded tub, and label it "food" for all nonperishable items.

- Large groups or families may want to have three labeled tubs for breakfast, lunch/snacks, and dinner/dessert.

- To be superorganized, group together items for each meal and place in large zip-top or grocery bags.

- Put cans on the bottom, squishables like bread on top.

PACKING A COOLER
Keeping perishables cold is an important safety rule to follow

When it's just the two of you camping, a medium-sized, soft-sided cooler is usually enough. But some couples tend toward minimalism.

Instead of buying bags of ice, freeze foods and water bottles to keep food cold. Use up fresh food in the first few days, then use up dry and canned foods for the last few days.

But when you go camping with friends or family members, you will need to take more and to cook more complicated meals. That's when it's great to haul out the big hard-sided cooler on wheels.

It's important to have a good cooler with good insulation, a drain plug, and one or two bins for smaller items you don't want soaking in melted ice.

You may want a second, smaller cooler to store cold drinks

Safe Packing Principles

- Put raw meat in watertight containers.
- Do the same with vegetables so they aren't sitting in contaminated water.
- Replenish ice daily.
- Freeze water bottles, which can be drunk as the ice melts.
- Use the tray for smaller or softer items.

Watertight Containers

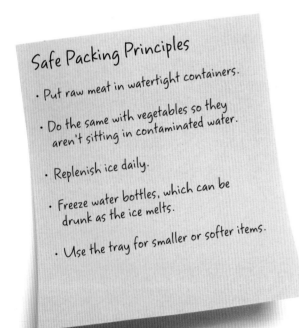

Look for a locking latch.

- Keep thawing meat juices from contaminating other food.

- Put raw meat and vegetables in watertight containers or zip-top bags.

- Keeping food in its original container will help keep it watertight.

- Reserve space for a zip-top bag of things that melt in hot weather: lipstick, crayons, and chocolate.

or to keep in the back seat of the car. A small soft-sided cooler is nice for packing a lunch as well.

If you have perishables like meat, mayonnaise, and dairy, put some thought into packing and restocking the cooler with ice to make them last and to prevent anyone from getting sick.

ZOOM

To prolong the life of your ice: Freeze food and drinks if possible. Put food in first, then cover with ice. Keep the cooler out of the sun, and keep it covered with a wet towel. Avoid frequent opening, and close the lid tight. Don't drain all the cold water. Keep meats/perishables directly on ice.

A cooler like this one, with vertical sides, means less wasted space.

Camp Fridge

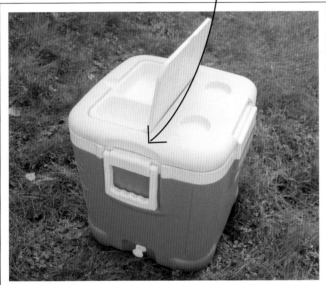

- Be sure the cooler has good insulation, a drain plug, and one or two trays.

- Save your back by getting a cooler on wheels with a long handle.

- Be sure the lid closes snugly. Some models have a locking lid to keep critters or little hands out.

- Discourage browsing in the cooler by having a separate smaller cooler for cold drinks. Freeze these ahead to make them last even longer on hot days.

Refilling Ice

- Try to replenish ice daily and drain water.

- If you can't replenish ice daily, do not drain. The cold water will still help insulate.

- Pour food on top of ice.

- Consider a block of ice in the bottom of the cooler. It lasts longer than cubes.

LOADING THE CAR

Use the building block method when packing your vehicle with supplies

Having lived out of our Subaru wagon for months on end, it's safe to say we've become experts on packing a car.

All the camping gear, clothes, and food go in the back cargo area. The backseat is the mobile office with a milk crate of reference books, two laptop computer cases, and a box of files with maps and brochures on each destination to be visited.

A watertight container holds electronics like GPS, phone chargers, and extra batteries right behind the driver's seat. We should say that Bill is the expert on packing the car. We learned early on it is best to have one chief packer: Packing by committee doesn't work.

Assemble all the gear at the car before beginning to pack.

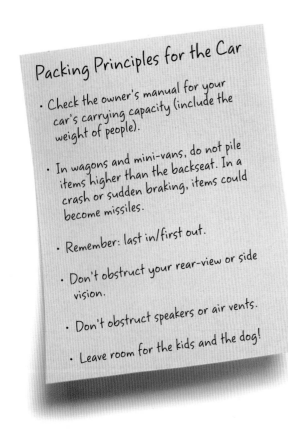

Packing Principles for the Car

• Check the owner's manual for your car's carrying capacity (include the weight of people).

• In wagons and mini-vans, do not pile items higher than the backseat. In a crash or sudden braking, items could become missiles.

• Remember: last in/first out.

• Don't obstruct your rear-view or side vision.

• Don't obstruct speakers or air vents.

• Leave room for the kids and the dog!

First/Last

• Grab the tent set-up and kitchen gear tubs right away, and start setting up the kitchen and bedroom before it gets dark. These tubs should go in last.

• Consider that you might not arrive in the best weather conditions or that it may be getting dark, so

have rain gear and flashlights at the ready.

• That said, you should place heavy items directly behind the backseat to prevent shifting.

• Use lighter items like pillows and pads to fill up the spaces around heavier items.

68

Use the building block method of stacking and fitting things together like a puzzle. Put things in last that you'll need to get out first: tent and kitchen set-up tubs.

It helps to practice well before departure time to be sure everything will fit. Too much? Time to get a rooftop carrier (see page 70 for this and carrying kayaks and bikes on your car).

(see page 70 for this and carrying kayaks and bikes on your car).

YELLOW ● LIGHT

Always leave room for the "oops" factor: the bag of snacks on the kitchen counter, the box of shoes, the backpack, the four stuffed animals that the child absolutely can't leave home without. You don't want to find out at the last minute that there's not enough room for the dog or the kids!

Driving Kit

- There are many things to keep handy while driving. The temptation is to pack too much in the front console and cause overcrowding.

- Necessities are a driving map, water bottle, tissues, hand wipes, and sunglasses.

- If you have room behind the front seat, keep a small cooler of drinks and a bag of snacks.

- For roadside breakdowns, be aware you may need to unload the cargo area to get at a spare tire, tool kit, or jumper cables.

Backseat Kit

- Have a small cooler of drinks/snacks in the backseat and some pillows for resting.

- Have a fun box or bag of games, books, videos, and crayons.

- A jump rope or ball is a good item to help expel some energy on rest stops.

- Before packing a lot of gear around child seats, be sure that they are properly secured and that all necessary seatbelts are accessible and working.

CARTOP CARRIERS

When everything you want to bring won't fit inside, consider a roof-top carrier

Luggage and roof racks enable you to bring all kinds of recreational and extra gear, whether it's a stroller and playpen, or bikes, skis, surfboard, boogie board, fishing poles, kayak, or canoe.

Soft luggage carriers can strap directly to your roof. But you need to have an installed roof rack with luggage bars to attach after-market racks for specific gear like kayaks, bikes, and skis.

Fishing poles even can be put in long PVC containers and strapped to a roof rack.

In addition, a platform off the back of the car that slips into an existing receiver hitch can carry coolers and lawn chairs put in the receiver hitch.

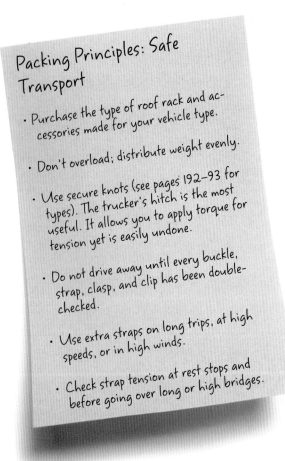

Packing Principles: Safe Transport

• Purchase the type of roof rack and accessories made for your vehicle type.

• Don't overload; distribute weight evenly.

• Use secure knots (see pages 192–93 for types). The trucker's hitch is the most useful. It allows you to apply torque for tension yet is easily undone.

• Do not drive away until every buckle, strap, clasp, and clip has been double-checked.

• Use extra straps on long trips, at high speeds, or in high winds.

• Check strap tension at rest stops and before going over long or high bridges.

Luggage Carriers

• Soft bag carriers of waterproof fabric can attach to the roof even without a roof rack.

• Put lighter items like bedding and clothing in a bag carrier so you don't dent the roof of your car.

• An aerodynamic, rigid, box luggage carrier that attaches to the roof rack can hold slightly heavier and harder objects.

• Do not exceed the manufacturer's weight limit.

However, great care must be taken with all these methods of carrying objects on the outside of your car. Luggage racks have been known to fly off a vehicle if overloaded. If not secured properly, bikes or kayaks can come flying off and become deadly missiles to other drivers.

Think worst case scenario and take measures to prevent it. Consider a lock for your carrier if you plan on leaving your car unattended.

ZOOM

It's all in the straps. Sturdy nylon straps with locking grips and even tension ratchets are preferred to rope. They are available at auto and marine stores. Straps are subject to UV exposure and chafing, so they should be checked for wear and tear before every trip.

With a trunk mount, be sure the bike's pedals do not rub the vehicle's paint.

Bike Racks

- Bike racks can be mounted on the trunk, roof, or a receiver hitch.

- The least expensive and simplest is the trunk mount, which attaches via straps and hooks.

- Rooftop bike racks attach to the car's luggage rack.

Always be aware of the height of your vehicle plus the bikes.

- Receiver hitch racks slide easily into your car's hitch mount. However, it's difficult to get into the trunk.

Kayaks and Canoes

- Plastic boats can rest directly on the luggage rack, perhaps cushioned with foam blocks.

- Cradle attachments are preferable for more expensive fiberglass or Kevlar boats.

- On long trips or in windy conditions, strap boats to the vehicle as well as to the roof rack, using bow and stern lines or a long strap that goes around everything.

- Don't use boats for extra storage, or else you may exceed the recommended weight for your luggage rack.

PITCHING THE TENT

Set it up right the first time to avoid hassle later

In our car camping experience, there have been a few very memorable nights when we had to get up in the middle of the night and move the tent. Once, it was because we were perched on a high sand dune facing the setting sun. It seemed like a good idea until the wind picked up in the middle of the night, blowing sand through the zippers and threatening to blow us away! Fortunately, we had a free-standing tent, so we pulled up the tent stakes, picked up the tent, and moved it to a sheltered spot.

While you should use an established tent pad if there is one, sometimes you have a choice of spots. Tent position is important for comfort, safety, as well as aesthetics. Stay away from low ground where rain might puddle. Avoid pitching under a lone tall tree in case lightning comes up. Position the

Choosing a Tent Site

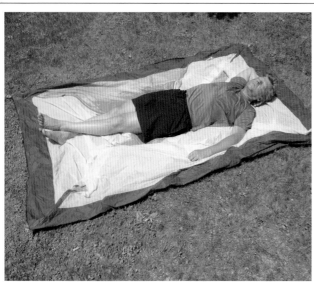

- A tent pad or an obvious existing spot for the tent.

- If not, look for a level spot, avoiding low ground that may flood if it rains.

- Spread the ground cloth first, being sure it is a few inches smaller all around than the tent body.

- Lie down to be sure that the ground is level and that there are no rocks or sticks that can cause discomfort or damage the tent floor.

- Pitch the tent so doors and vents are aligned with the wind direction for maximum ventilation.

Poles

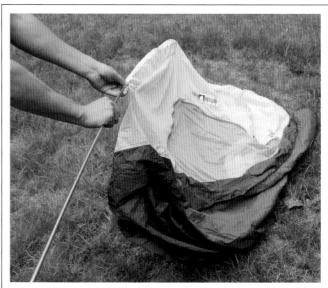

- Today's tent poles are usually several pieces of aluminum tubing connected with shock cord.

- Although poles can withstand pressure and bending after the tent is set up, the joints are actually quite fragile.

- Assemble the poles gently, and do not leave them lying on the ground to step on.

- After they are assembled, feed them carefully through the tent tunnels to prevent ripping the tent fabric.

door for a morning sunrise or water view.

Above all, you need to be familiar with setting up your tent quickly. Have the family practice at home. A backyard sleep-out can be a fun start to a camping adventure.

Use a rubber mallet to pound stakes if ground is hard or rocky.

Grommets and Stakes

- Gently flex the poles and insert the tips into the appropriate grommets, and then the tent body will be erect.

- There are often clips on the tent body that snap onto the poles for added stability.

- The second set of grommets is for the tent stakes. Press stakes into the ground with your hand or foot.

- Before staking, you can move a freestanding tent for optimum placement.

Rain Fly

- The rain fly is like a rain coat: It's waterproof to repel rain but allows ventilation into the tent.

- The rain fly usually clips in via buckles or hooks near the base of the poles.

- The rain fly should be staked out at a 45 degree angle to allow ventilation and to prevent it from touching the tent body and allowing moisture to get in.

- In high winds achieve additional stability via staked guy lines or tie to nearby trees or rocks.

CAMP KITCHEN
Have one chief chef who delegates jobs to other family members

One of the secrets to cooking well and efficiently outdoors is to spend time organizing the kitchen before you light the stove.

Just as we've found it better to have one person in charge of packing the car, it works most efficiently to have a king (or queen) of the kitchen. The head cook will know how he or she wants things set up.

That's not to say he or she does all the work, not by any means! Parcel out jobs such as gathering wood and starting a fire if you are having a fire, fetching water, unloading gear, washing and chopping vegetables, and setting the table.

Decide immediately where the camp kitchen should be before you start unloading gear helter skelter.

The kitchen should be as far as possible from where you

Organize Food and Gear

- Use one end of the picnic table to set up your stove. Place kitchen gear tub, cooler, and food tubs on the ends of the benches.

- Put anything you don't need back in the car or, better yet, don't bring it out at all.

- Open the cooler as little as possible to grab what you need.

- Locate the lantern, matches, and flashlights before it gets dark.

Tarp

Be sure the tarp is taut, with no sags to collect rain.

- If there's a chance of rain, you might want to set the tarp over the picnic table before setting up the kitchen. An easy-up canopy is another option.

- Both provide shade as well as rain protection.

- Use reflective cord for guy lines to prevent tripping at night.

- Unlike car loading and kitchen set-up, tarp or canopy set-up is a group effort, made easiest with four people, one at each corner.

sleep for two reasons: fire and critters.

There might not be a lot of choice if there's a set tent pad or if the picnic table is chained down. But if possible, set up a triangular system of where you cook, sleep, and make a fire.

Before it gets dark, set up the tarp for rain and/or sun protection.

Stove Set-up

- Most people set up their stove at one end of a picnic table.

- Be sure the stove is on a nonflammable, nonmeltable surface.

- If you have a freestanding camp stove or grill, be sure it is on level ground.

- If children are about, you may want to set up your tubs to create a U-shaped cooking area to keep them away from the hot stove.

Water

- Soon after arriving, assign someone to locate the nearest water supply and fill a jug or collapsible container.

- Set up a plastic wash basin or foldable camp sink in anticipation of dinner clean-up, which could come after dark. Locate the dish soap and sponge and set it nearby.

- Top off individual water bottles for nighttime sipping.

- Be sure there's enough water for the morning coffee and breakfast prep.

COMFORTS OF HOME
There's no need to rough it when car camping

Camping shouldn't be about deprivation. Small luxuries are important because they remind you of home, which can make first-time or reluctant campers feel more secure.

Bring your favorite quilt or afghan to throw around your shoulders while sitting around the fire on a chilly night.

String up a tarp in case it rains, and you'll have a dry place to cook, read, or play cards. Pillows are really important in the tent, as are favorite stuffed toys, which create a sense of familiarity for the young ones.

Make the tent a cozy nest: If the site is slightly inclined, be sure your heads are at the high end. Arrange the pillows, using duffel bags for additional height. Place books, headlamps, and water bottles near your head within reach in the dark.

In essence, make the campsite your outdoor living room,

Before It Gets Dark

- Make the "beds" by inflating the air mattresses and arranging and zipping up the sleeping bags.

- Be sure there's enough water for nighttime sips and morning coffee.

- Set up the lantern and be sure there are flashlights handy in the tent for bathroom visits.

- Take these items inside the tent at night: flashlight/headlamp, car keys, cell phone, tissue packet, water bottle, book to read.

Fire Circle

- Appoint one or more people to gather and organize wood for a campfire.

- Arrange piles of wood by size (match-size twigs, pencil-size twigs, wrist-size limbs).

- Locate the matches and newspaper, hatchet, and saw.

- Place chairs around the circle. Start to talk to children about fire safety before the fire is lit.

with sitting, cooking, and play areas.

Stick to some of your favorite evening rituals, whether it's having a mini-facial, brushing your teeth and flossing, or reading aloud to each other.

Camp Seating

- Avoid sitting on the cold, hard ground. If you have no chairs at all, bring out your air mattress to sit around the fire.

- A variety of camp chairs is on the market, from lightweight stadium seats to folding umbrellas chairs. Older people, however, may have difficulty getting up from the Crazy Creek-style seats.

- Or simply bring your beach chairs or lawn chairs from home.

- String up a hammock in the shade, or spread out a blanket to create a play area for small children.

Screen Room

- A freestanding screen room provides a cozy place to sit in the shade and away from insects.

- Bugs always seem to know when it's dinnertime, so set it up well before you are ready to sit down to eat.

- Even though the label may say the screen room is nonflammable, don't cook inside. Carbon monoxide can accumulate (never cook in a tent either).

- Be sure the fabric is taut: Sagging will result in pooling rain.

VARMINTPROOFING
Any food or trash will attract insects and animals

Many think it's cute to feed chipmunks or raccoons. After all, what harm does it do?

However, animals who become habituated to human contact and acquaint human presence with food eventually become nuisance animals. If they become too aggressive they may have to be trapped and relocated or even euthanized. An aggressive bear is a danger to humans as well.

The degree of critterproofing depends on your location. In the West you may have to worry about grizzly bears or mountain lions.

But even smaller critters, like raccoons, can ruin your camping trip. These deft animals can open a tub or cooler quite easily and carry away a good bit of food in a matter of minutes. From personal experience, we've known them to steal

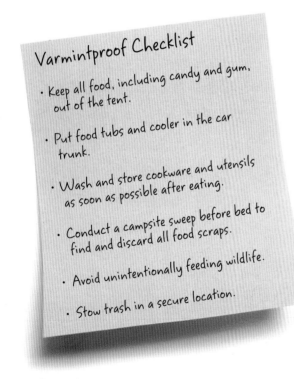

Varmintproof Checklist

- Keep all food, including candy and gum, out of the tent.
- Put food tubs and cooler in the car trunk.
- Wash and store cookware and utensils as soon as possible after eating.
- Conduct a campsite sweep before bed to find and discard all food scraps.
- Avoid unintentionally feeding wildlife.
- Stow trash in a secure location.

Stow Food

- Always close food tubs when not in use.

- Ants are notoriously quick and will get into your zip-top bag of sugar in a matter of minutes. Habituated raccoons have no qualms about joining you for dinner.

- Right after dinner, stow food tub and cooler in trunk of car.

- Clean up the dishes right away and put trash either in the trunk or in a Dumpster. Smells quickly attract animals, especially nocturnal ones.

toothpaste and even vitamins.

Latch coolers, and strap down food tubs with bungee cords when not in use. They should be stowed in the car as soon as possible after meals.

During meal prep, avoid letting crumbs fall beneath the table while chopping food. During mealtime, always use a plate, or eat standing over water, which will carry crumbs away.

Treat trash like food; to critters it is just as appetizing.

Backpackers should always hang their food in a bear bag.

Hang Food

- If for some reason you can't or don't want to stow food in your car, hang a bag to protect it from bears and raccoons.

- Put all your food into a ditty or duffel bag, tie a rope around the top, and sling the rope over an overhanging branch or from a metal hook provided in some campsites.

- Be sure it hangs high enough from the trunk of the tree so that a clever animal can't reach it.

- Check to be sure that hanging something from trees is allowed in your particular campground.

Specially made canisters are impervious to even the most dexterous animals.

Bear Canister

- This is primarily for grizzly bear country and places where black bears have become very aggressive.

- Most often your food and trash are safe in your car. But large bears have been known to break out auto glass if they can see and/or smell food.

- Most likely the campground will make you aware of this danger and recommend you put your food in a bear-proof canister.

- You may even want to change the clothes you cook in and not bring them into the tent for fear that the odor will attract bears.

SPECIAL CONDITIONS
Certain conditions require special camp set-up

Beach, winter, primitive, alpine, and desert conditions present rewards and challenges for the camper.

The typical campsite is a shady wooded setting, with a clear, level spot for the tent, a picnic table, and perhaps a fire ring or grill.

But in the real world of camping you'll likely encounter conditions that aren't as consistent. Some campgrounds, especially popular ones, may have an overflow tent area or primitive walk-in sites.

You'll have to carry all your gear a few hundred feet, but it could bring the reward of a deep woods experience and become the start of a passion for backpacking.

The sounds of the surf pounding or coyotes lulling you to sleep, nighttime beach walks, or sunrise over the desert:

Beach Camping

If there are no dunes, set up well above the high tide line.

- Use established sites, if available. If not, set up behind beach dunes but not on them.

- Sand stakes are a must. They are made of aluminum or titanium, are usually longer than 10 inches, and sometimes have spiral grooves for better grip.

- Take some special precautions for windproofing your site because there are no natural structures to buffer wind.

- The sun will be beating down all day long. Keep a wet towel over the cooler and set up a tarp for shade.

Winter Camping

Tent anchor sacks, filled with rocks or snow, hold better than stakes.

- Have warm weather gear, a four-season tent, and sleeping bags rated to the lowest temperature.

- Even if you don't intend to camp in winter conditions, occasionally an early spring or late autumn snow may surprise you, especially at higher elevations.

- Don't panic. If a squall brings heavy snow, be sure to keep it from building up on top of the tent by brushing it off periodically.

- Bring along some snowshoes or cross-country skis for trekking in the woods.

These are special pleasures of camping on the beach or in the desert. Without shade, you'll likely want a tarp or screen room for protection from sun and wind.

Some hardy souls love the uniqueness of winter camping. Awaking to absolute quiet after a snowfall can be a real treat. Look for animal tracks in the fresh snow.

Set up stove and lantern on nonflammable surfaces.

Primitive Camping

- Occasionally you may want to or need to camp in a primitive or walk-in site.

- First, locate the nearest water supply and bathroom or outhouse to determine how far you'll need to walk. Fetch water before it gets dark.

- If there isn't a bathroom, you'll need to inform everyone in the group on environmentally sound practices for going to the bathroom and washing dishes (see Chapter 10, Zero Impact).

- In the absence of a picnic table, set up the stove on a flat rock, bare ground, or sand to avoid starting a grassfire.

Sensitive Environments

- When camping in wilderness areas, in desertlike climates, or above the tree line, minimize all human impact and do not build fires.

- In the absence of established campsites, camp so that when you leave there will be no sign of your presence.

- Do not cut or clear brush, move rocks, or alter the site in any way.

- General Leave No Trace practices may not suffice here. Check local regulations, but you may have to pack out all human waste (no digging catholes or even peeing on the ground allowed).

FOOD PREPARATION
Make food preparation an organized, fun time

If you're not rushed by impending dark or threatening clouds, make food prep an event. It's community/family time that can be spent bonding with others and really getting in the camping spirit. Food always seems to taste better outdoors.

For the kitchen king or queen, this is your chance to shine. Perhaps someone else is setting up the tent while the kids are gathering firewood, giving you a quiet moment to form a game plan for dinner.

You'll likely bring your at-home methods and shortcuts to camp. Perhaps you've started food prep earlier in the day at camp or even at home by marinating some meat for the grill.

If you've frozen any ingredients, pull them out to finish thawing.

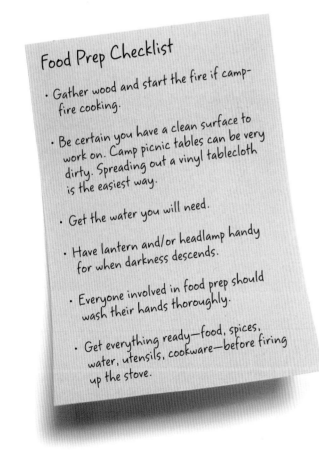

Food Prep Checklist

- Gather wood and start the fire if camp-fire cooking.

- Be certain you have a clean surface to work on. Camp picnic tables can be very dirty. Spreading out a vinyl tablecloth is the easiest way.

- Get the water you will need.

- Have lantern and/or headlamp handy for when darkness descends.

- Everyone involved in food prep should wash their hands thoroughly.

- Get everything ready—food, spices, water, utensils, cookware—before firing up the stove.

Clean Hands

- Everyone participating in meal prep should have clean hands.

- Wash hands in soap and warm water, heating it on the stove, if necessary. In the absence of warm running water, use hand sanitizer.

- Rub vigorously for at least twenty seconds, including backs of hands, wrists, between fingers, and under fingernails.

- Rinse in running water; dry with a clean towel.

Think of tasks for little helpers. Most kids love to help cook, but they lose interest quickly if they don't have a task.

Of course, breakfast and lunch may not require as much preparation, but even just a little bit of prep time can be fun.

If a day of activity is planned, make lunch ahead of time. Right after breakfast, get in the habit of pulling out the ingredients and making lunch sandwiches so you don't have to haul out the food twice.

Chopping Food

- Start with at least two good sharp knives, one for paring/peeling and a larger one for chopping.

- Chop on a clean surface—a cutting board or plate—not on the picnic table.

- Keep raw meat and juices away from vegetables.

- Thoroughly clean knife and cutting board used for raw meat.

- Have a bowl, plate, or skillet handy to slide chopped food into.

Organization Is Key

- If you've packed correctly (see pages 64–67), it should be easy to pull out exactly what you need for each meal.

- Set up stations for peeling, chopping, and opening cans with the food and required utensils. Then call over some helpers.

- If you're having a fire for grilling or Dutch oven cooking, be sure someone starts it early enough.

- Get everything assembled and chopped before you light the stove.

USING A CAMP STOVE

Become familiar with the peculiarities of your camp stove

Give yourself a bit more time to cook outdoors. The time it takes to cook meals on your camp stove may be different from the time it takes on your home stove. Camp stoves often take longer to boil water, for instance.

Also, stoves vary widely in fuel consumption, heat output, simmer control, and cold weather performance.

If your stove is new, it's not a bad idea to test a meal in the backyard first. Heat control is usually not as refined as on a home stove, so experiment to find the correct settings for boiling, frying, sautéing, and low simmering without burning or overflowing.

Old fuel will not burn cleanly, causing weak or surging flame. The flame should be blue. If it is orange and sporadic, you may have a clogged fuel line or old fuel.

Stove Safety Checklist

- Always set a stove on a level surface.
- Never leave a stove unattended.
- Never sit down in front of a stove.
- Never reach across a lit stove.
- Keep children well away from a lit stove and hot pots.
- Never cook inside a tent.
- Don't put large pots on a single-burner stove, or else they may topple.

Stove Set-up

Windscreens are vital for efficient heating.

- Locate a flat, level surface for your cooking area.

- If using the end of the picnic table, place some tubs or coolers on either side to prevent children from getting too close.

- Open the suitcase stove and set up the side windscreen flaps.

- If setting up on the ground, use a flat rock or an area of dirt or gravel. Use large stones around a single-burner stove for support.

Position the stove at the end of the picnic table so you can stand in front of it.

Never sit in front of a stove, whether it's on the ground or a picnic table. In the event of hot liquids spillage, you need to react quickly to move away.

ZOOM

Lighting a liquid fuel stove: Assemble the stove and windscreen, and attach fuel bottle. Pump the fuel bottle to create pressure. Prime by turning the knob just long enough to allow a small pool of fuel to collect in the priming cup. Light the fuel, and allow it to burn off. Turn the fuel knob, and light the stove. Flame should burn steady blue. While cooking, the flame may decrease, requiring more pumping.

Don't turn the knob until the match is lit.

Attaching the Fuel Container

- For propane stoves, screw the fuel hose fitting onto the canister or tank, being careful to match the threads.

- Single-burner stoves screw directly onto the canister.

- For liquid-fuel stoves slide the pin into the bottle's receiver.

- Refill liquid-fuel bottles away from gear and food, and be sure the caps are secure when traveling.

Lighting the Stove

- Light the stove only when you are ready to put a pot of food on the burner.

- Light the match or lighter and hold it with one hand. With the other turn the knob slowly until you hear the hiss of propane.

- If the match or lighter goes out before the burner is lit, turn the knob completely off immediately, and try again.

- The burner closest to the fuel burns the hottest, so reserve it for tasks requiring high heat, such as boiling water.

COOKING TECHNIQUES

With just a little effort, camp food can be savory and satisfying

Even if you're not a gourmet, there's no need for food to be boring in the outdoors. Even one-pot and dehydrated meals can be spiced up with fresh or canned meat, vegetables, or legumes.

Plan to eat meals using fresh ingredients or raw meat early in the trip, paying special attention to safe food handling and refrigeration in the outdoors.

Canned vegetables are nonperishable and convenient, but fresher taste better and are better for you. Vegetables like carrots, potatoes, squash, onions, cauliflower, and cabbage last longer and usually don't need refrigeration if the outdoor temperature isn't too hot. Do keep in mind that root vegetables take longer to cook.

Timing can be tricky when you're away from your home

Make Just Enough

- Follow the package recommendations for portions, then add a third. Most people eat more in the outdoors.

- One pound of dry food feeds about three people.

- One portion of meat or cooked grain is about the size of your fist. Hence, larger people get larger portions.

- Be sure to measure.

- Save extra rice to make rice pudding for dessert or breakfast.

One-pot Meals

- Be sure to include protein, grain, and vegetable for a complete, tasty, one-pot meal.

- Dress up a pre-packaged pasta or rice dish with a can of peas, corn, beans, or chopped kielbasa, ham, canned chicken, or tuna.

- Brown fresh meat, onions, and garlic in the bottom of the pot, then add other ingredients to make stew or chili.

- Cook pasta or rice, drain, then add sauce to let the hot grain heat it up.

stove. Be sure to have a watch. Give a little thought to having dishes done about the same time. Add cooking time at higher altitudes.

Although we all tend to eat more when we're outdoors, try to make just enough for the group's needs. Leftovers don't do well in a cooler, and food trash attracts animals.

One-pot meals make clean-up a breeze.

ZOOM

Your spice and condiment kits are key (see page 32) to creating tasty camp meals. Learn which seasonings complement which foods, or buy pre-mixed seasoning packets for meat, fish, poultry, pasta, or soup. Ethnic seasoning packets, such as for Thai or Mexican food, are readily available. Fresh garlic cloves travel and keep very well and add much flavor, far superior to garlic salt.

Double Burner

- Create a double burner over a single-burner stove to cook meals more efficiently.

- Heat sauce by flipping over the pot lid and setting it atop boiling pasta or rice.

- Put a smaller pot inside a larger one that has a few inches of water in it.

- This type of double boiler can prevent burning fragile foods like melting cheese or chocolate.

Skillet Meals

- The concept of Hamburger Helper is great for one-skillet meals in camp.

- First, brown meat, onions, and garlic, add quick-cooking rice or pasta and water, and simmer.

- Next, add vegetables based on the time they take to cook.

- Add soft vegetables, like mushrooms, and tofu last so they don't overcook.

CATCHING YOUR OWN FOOD

A little know-how and technique will make you nearly self-sufficient in the wilds

There are some campers who go on three- or four-day camping trips with a fishing pole and very little food. Those campers are pretty confident in their fishing abilities! But it's not a great idea to rely on catching your own food unless you're adept at it and know what the environment will yield.

There are plenty of other wild foods that you can "catch" out in the field or in the woods in spring and summer.

For example, we once had the treat of going on a wild foraged food hike with clinical herbalist Teresa Boardwine on the edge of Virginia's Blue Ridge Mountains.

On a leisurely woods walk, we learned of all the delicious and nutritious "weeds" beneath our feet. Within thirty min-

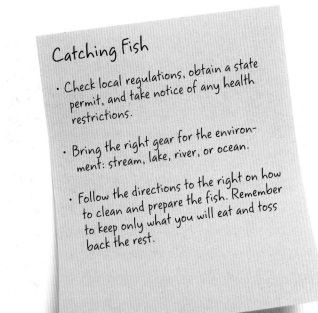

Catching Fish

- Check local regulations, obtain a state permit, and take notice of any health restrictions.

- Bring the right gear for the environment: stream, lake, river, or ocean.

- Follow the directions to the right on how to clean and prepare the fish. Remember to keep only what you will eat and toss back the rest.

The First Cut

- There are many ways to fillet a fish, depending on personal style and the type of fish.

- Here's a simple method that removes the skin (no need for scaling) and leaves the abdominal cavity intact (no need to remove the innards).

- You'll need a sharp fillet knife and a garbage bag for waste. Place fish on cutting board.

- Just behind the gills, cut the head to the bone, flip it over, and cut the other side. Leaving the head on gives you a handle while filleting.

KNACK CAR CAMPING FOR EVERYONE

88

utes we had picked enough for a stir-fry dinner of burdock root, ramps (a wild onion that's everywhere), morel mushrooms, and fiddlehead ferns.

We made a chickweed, chive, and violet blossom butter, a pesto of garlic mustard (an invasive nonnative that needs to be pulled up anyway!), and lemon balm and mint tea.

We were pleasantly, and surprisingly, full. Now we know that at least in the springtime, we'll never go hungry on the trail—or look at the weeds in our lawn quite the same way again!

• • • • • • • • • • • • • • • • RED ● LIGHT • • • • • • • • • • • • •

Eat wild foods only if you're 100 percent sure of their identity and safety. Getting a handbook on wild edibles is a good idea. These wild foods are easy to cook with and safe to identify: blueberries, raspberries, blackberries, ramps (wild scallion), dandelion, violets, and fiddlehead ferns.

Fillet the Fish

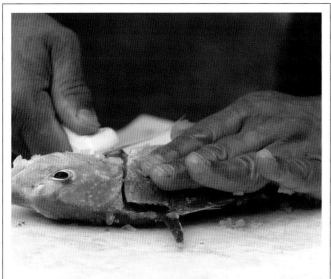

- Run the knife along the backbone and dorsal fin.

- Knife should go deep enough to glide along but not through the ribcage bones.

- Continue cutting along the bone until the fillet is cut off at the tail.

- Flip the fish over and repeat on other side.

Remove Skin

- Insert the knife at the tail end of the fillet, parallel to the cutting board.

- Holding the skin with one thumb, slide the knife close to the skin to keep as much meat as possible. Repeat on other fillet.

- Rinse off any blood, and you're ready to bread and fry or grill your fish with butter and lemon.

- Dispose of fish waste properly so it doesn't attract animals.

MEALTIME

CAMP DINING
Just a few comfort items can make mealtime memorable

Some of the most memorable camp meals are mobile picnics. After cooking, grab your seats, headlamps, plates of food, and a bottle of wine, and head to a ridge-top perch, mountain view, or to a lakeside, streamside, or beach to watch the sunset for a couple's retreat.

For big family dinners, when sitting down to dine with friends and family at the picnic table, create a little ambience with lighting, napkins, and a fun tablecloth—just like a fancy dinner at home.

It's key that all the prep food, cooking utensils, and cutting boards have been cleared and put away prior to sitting down to an uncluttered table.

When it gets dark, light a lantern and some citronella candles to keep the bugs down while you enjoy your meal. It's

Dining Checklist
- Tablecloth and napkins
- Lighting
- Personal mess kits or table settings
- Serving utensils
- Pads, folded towel, flat rock for hot pots
- Be sure stove is off.
- Put food away prior to sitting down.

Table Lighting

- Propane lanterns, like a one-burner stove, screw easily onto a disposable canister. Be sure to have extra lantern mantles in case one breaks.

- Candles create ambience, keep bugs away, and don't use fuel.

- A headlamp is great for hands-free lighting, but your tablemates don't want the beam shining in their eyes. Instead, position a headlamp against a colored water bottle for some mood lighting.

- Battery-operated lanterns are the easiest to use.

good to have the bug spray nearby; bugs seem to always come out at dinnertime.

Don't rush mealtime. Sit for hours, talking, laughing, sipping wine, perhaps playing cards with friends and family, much like you'd do at dinner parties at home.

Cloth napkins add a touch of elegance and reduce waste.

Simple

- The minimalist needs little more than plate, spork, and a place to sit.

- Spread a blanket on the grass or position seats for optimum views of lake, mountain, or sunset.

- Don't leave food or trash unattended at camp. Raccoons are fast.

- Don't forget to put on a headlamp in anticipation of dark.

Gourmet

- Cover the picnic table with a vinyl or cloth table covering.

- Light candles to provide ambience and to keep bugs away. Citronella works well.

- Stow the food tubs and cooler before you sit down. There's nothing worse than having uninvited guests crash your dinner party!

- Have bug spray, playing cards, and water bottles handy.

MEALTIME

CLEAN-UP
Quick and efficient clean-up will leave more time for fun and will keep critters away

The keys to easy clean-up are to do it soon after eating and to try to eat all the leftover food. Encourage seconds or thirds if you have to! Scrape excess food into the trash and roll up your sleeves.

For gunky pots and pans, especially with burned food in the bottom, make life easier for the clean-up crew: Pour a few inches of water into the pot, then place it on the stove to loosen some of the food debris.

If there is a tub sink at the bathhouse, simply carry all the dirty dishes there in a bucket or dishpan. Scrap food particles from the bottom of the pot into the trash to prevent the sink from clogging. If there isn't such a sink, please do not use the

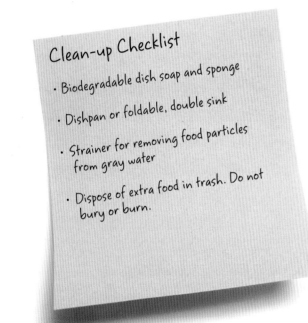

Clean-up Checklist
• Biodegradable dish soap and sponge
• Dishpan or foldable, double sink
• Strainer for removing food particles from gray water
• Dispose of extra food in trash. Do not bury or burn.

Tub Sink

Please scrape plates into trash can not into sink

- If the campground provides tub sinks at the bathhouse, use them.

- Do not use the bathroom sinks because food clogs drains and causes a mess for others.

- A small dishpan is handy for taking dirty dishes, soap, and sponge to the bathhouse.

- Dry with a towel or air dry by placing upside down in the clean dishpan or in mesh ditty bags.

bathroom sink! It can make an unappealing mess for the next person trying to brush his teeth.

If you need to clean up at camp, heat some water over the stove and use two dishpans or pots: one for washing and the other for rinsing. Never rinse under a spigot. Broadcast strained gray water at least 200 feet from your campsite. Always follow the Zero Impact practices mentioned below.

Cleaning at Campsite

- If the campground does not have a tub sink, you'll have to wash up at your campsite.

- Never wash directly under a spigot. Food particles and water puddles create a mess for others and attract animals.

- Heat water on the stove, and pour it into a dishpan with some biodegradable soap.

- Rinse in clean water and either towel dry or allow to air dry on the picnic table or in mesh ditty bags.

Broadcast Gray Water

- Even if you wash dishes at camp, you should still take the dirty dishwater to the bathhouse and dump it down the toilet.

- If primitive camping where there are no sinks or toilets, use the Zero Impact process for disposing of dishwater:

- You must first remove food particles by pouring the water through a strainer, catching the gray water in another container.

- Broadcast the gray water by flinging the pot or tub so that the water spreads out over a large area.

LOW-IMPACT FIRES
Consider if you really need to build a fire at all

It's a camping tradition, but fire does impact the environment. It can scar the landscape and deplete dead and downed wood, which is important for some life-forms. Of course, if the weather is windy, or if fires are prohibited, absolutely do not build one.

Make an evening around the fire a treat, not something you do every night. Sitting around telling stories and cooking

s'mores is a time-honored camping tradition and fond childhood memory for many but should be considered a treat, not a regular event.

If you're out in the backcountry, and someone is getting hypothermic, building a fire can be a lifesaver. So, for safety reasons, you should know how to build a low-impact fire.

All fires should be contained in a fire ring of rock or metal, in

Keep It Small

- Bonfires are for movies and teenage parties, unfortunately.

- Keep a fire small and burning only for the time you are using it.

- Limit the size of branches to no larger than your wrist.

- Piling large logs or long limbs that extend past the fire ring is asking for trouble.

- Be aware that sparks from a large fire can fly quite far and ignite brush.

Fire Alternatives

- Use a fire pan with sides at least 3 inches high. Place it on rocks or mineral soil so the heat doesn't scorch the ground.

- In an emergency situation, to warm someone who is dangerously hypothermic, you can build a mound fire.

- Place a ground cloth or plastic trash bag on the ground to keep the ground from being scorched.

- Spread mineral soil, sand, or gravel 3 to 5 inches thick on the plastic. Build a small fire on the soil. The plastic allows easy clean-up of the ashes.

a barbecue, or in an outdoor fireplace. If there isn't one, don't alter the landscape by building your own fire ring. Use a fire pan or portable grill instead.

You should do most of your cooking with a stove, but if it's a special night and you're going to build a fire anyway, consider making dinner in a Dutch oven or a freestanding grill over the fire.

Fire's End

- Burn wood completely to a fine ash.

- Pour a pot of water over the ashes to be sure the fire is completely out.

- In established camp-grounds, fire ring clean-out is usually done as part of campground maintenance.

- If you are in a primitive area, scatter the remains of ash over a large area away from camp but only after the remains are completely cooled.

Portable Grill

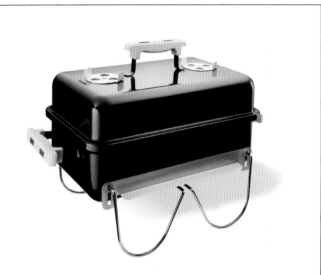

- A portable charcoal grill is another alternative to a campfire and even better for cooking.

- The grill can be close to the ground, rest on a picnic table like a hibachi, or be freestanding on a tripod.

- Coals are easier to place on top of a Dutch oven.

- There are built-in grills. Their heat is more efficient for grilling meat.

CAMPFIRES

BUILDING A FIRE
The thrill of victory, the agony of defeat

Wasn't it thrilling when Tom Hanks's character finally succeeded in making fire in the film *Cast Away*? As he danced around the roaring fire, half-clothed, we could all somehow relate to the primal excitement of life-giving fire.

The opposite is true when you've been blowing on wadded-up newspaper and smoky wet wood for an hour. There's nothing quite as debilitating among the camping scenarios.

The key is to start with seasoned, dried wood. Green, newly cut, or wet wood will not burn, and if it does it will burn slowly and produce a lot of smoke.

The best bet is to purchase a bundle at the camp store. Gathering wood around the campsite may be an option if it hasn't been picked over, or if you are in a sparsely populated national forest.

Gathering Fuel

- Even if you purchase a bundle of firewood, you'll still need some dry tinder.

- Use only dead and downed wood. Create three piles of different sizes of wood:

- Match-sized twigs, sticks about the diameter of a pencil, and wood about the diameter of an adult wrist.

- If wood is wet, whittle off the bark and wet wood until you reach the dry heartwood. Use these dry shavings as fire-starter, and slowly build a fire that will dry out the rest of your material.

Start with Tinder

Do not use gas to accelerate a fire.

- Dry, highly flammable tinder is the most important element in getting a blaze going.

- Tinder can be natural: wood shavings, dry leaves, or dead grass.

- Human-made materials that make good fire-starters include crumpled newspaper, food cartons, and paper bags.

- For nearly foolproof ignition, purchase some fire-starter sticks.

Gather wood only from the ground. Never cut or saw live trees. Even standing dead trees are homes for animals like pileated woodpeckers and small mammals.

Most importantly, be sure there are no seasonal fire restrictions and practice fire safety.

Start with a couple of forked sticks to support each other.

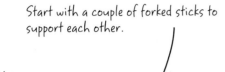

Construction

- Proper construction of the fire is key before you light the match.

- There are several designs, but we like the teepee style.

- Around a pile of tinder, start placing small sticks in increasing sizes, propping each other up like a teepee.

- Keep enough space so that air can flow through the tinder. Light tinder.

Feeding the Fire

- After the teepee gets going, you can start placing larger sticks on the fire, one at a time.

- Keep sticks no larger than the diameter of an adult's wrist.

- No wood should extend over the edge of the fire ring. Keep pushing the unburned ends of sticks into the flame.

- After the teepee collapses into a bed of hot coals you can cook over it.

CAMPFIRES

CAMPFIRE TIPS
Building a fire is not as simple as just lighting a match

Starting a fire is a challenge and a responsibility. Know the regulations as to whether fires are even allowed in the area. If the season has been particularly dry, there may be restrictions.

Even if there aren't restrictions, use common sense and don't build a fire in windy conditions. Teach children safety around fire and model good behavior yourself.

Once you're ready, there are some shortcuts to getting a good fire going. Don't be ashamed to buy fire starters or quick-start logs. Consider charcoal for cooking: it's more efficient and quicker to get coals than a wood fire. Keep your fire small: it's more efficient for cooking, will lessen the blackening of your pots, and allows you to get close enough to cook.

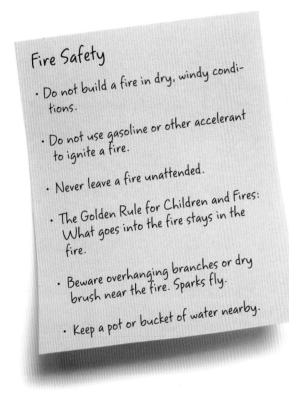

Fire Safety

- Do not build a fire in dry, windy conditions.

- Do not use gasoline or other accelerant to ignite a fire.

- Never leave a fire unattended.

- The Golden Rule for Children and Fires: What goes into the fire stays in the fire.

- Beware overhanging branches or dry brush near the fire. Sparks fly.

- Keep a pot or bucket of water nearby.

Fire Starters

For nearly foolproof ignition, purchase some fire starter sticks.

- Other good fire starters include crumpled newspaper, food cartons, dryer lint, or paper bags.

- Make your own firestarters:

- Put a piece of charcoal in each section of a paper egg carton. Tear apart and use as needed.

- Stuff toilet paper or paper towel rolls with newspaper.

If grilling meat or fish, have fun experimenting with different flavors from woods or charcoal mixes containing mesquite, cedar or hickory.

Never burn treated or painted lumber, as it will emit noxious fumes. Never burn trash--you do not know what chemicals are in packaging.

ZOOM

Prepare the campfire site: Always use a fire ring. It should be at least 10 feet away from logs, trees or debris that might catch fire. If the ring is already full of ashes or debris, shovel it out into a trash bag. Scrape down to the soil before building your fire. Keep a pail of water nearby.

Lighter fluid is usually necessary to get charcoal started.

Charcoal

- Charcoal and lighter fluid will create a nice bed of coals for cooking much more quickly than a wood fire.

- Pre-treated charcoal doesn't require lighter fluid.

- Consider natural lump charcoal, made of partially burned wood.

- Create different temperature zones on the grill by keeping the coals in one area and a cool zone in another.

Flavor

- Charcoal made of or mixed with specific woods gives barbecued meat different flavors.

- Hickory produces a sweet, hearty flavor.

- Mesquite results in a more smoky taste.

- Cooking on cedar planks has become popular of late, giving meat or fish a smoky flavor and letting it cook in its own juices.

CAMPFIRES

COOKING OVER A FIRE
Add a few techniques to your bag of tricks for easy campfire cooking

Cooking over an open fire does have its drawbacks: It blackens the cookware and takes longer than cooking over a stove, which lights in seconds. Fires also take a while to start. Most often after being out hiking all day, you arrive too late to gather wood, start a fire, and wait for the coals.

That said, cooking over an open fire is vividly memorable to many campers. Foods cooked over the open flame stick in one's head. Like the Dutch oven lasagna or the one-pot chili and cornbread meal. Or having kids make their own silver turtles, each sculpting the foil into whimsical shapes so they will know which is theirs.

What's more, grilled meat, chicken, or fish really takes on a splendid smoky flavor, and it's hard to make s'mores—a camping staple—without a fire.

Hot Bed of Coals

Wait until the fire has died down to hot coals.

- Cooking over a flaming fire is extremely inefficient, creates more soot on your pots, and can burn your fingers.

- There should be enough coals to last the amount of time your meal will take to cook. If not, add more wood and wait some more.

- If you'll be baking in a Dutch oven, be sure you have enough coals to cover the lid and to maintain the constant heat for the required time.

- If you're cooking food in foil or on a stick, you're ready to go.

Use a Grill

Use long-handled metal utensils.

- A freestanding grill placed over a bed of coals will provide a stable cooking area.

- Use pots and utensils that won't melt. Be aware of lids and handles of meltable material.

- Any cookware you use on a fire will become blackened, so use your oldest or camp-only cookware, not the ones you use at home.

- Try rubbing bar soap on the outside of the pot to ease clean-up. Place sooty pots in a plastic bag when packing for home.

You just can't be in a hurry. It takes time and patience to cook over a fire. But it can be worth it, in flavor and in memories.

Frying

- A griddle is a nice surface when cooking for a crowd or when you want to cook bacon and eggs at the same time.

- You don't have to worry about using cast iron on the fire: it's already black!

- A cast-iron skillet or griddle gives fish and meat a nice flavor, especially when it's rubbed with some Cajun seasoning.

- Consider wearing a pair of barbecue gloves or non-flammable work gloves to protect your hands.

Baking

Place coals on top of the flat lid.

- The one time we really advocate cooking over a fire is when baking with a Dutch oven.

- As described in earlier chapters, you can make desserts, breads, and one-pot dinners inside.

- The pot is nestled in the coals, and others are placed on top to simulate all-over oven baking.

- For easier clean-up, consider lining the oven with foil before filling it with food.

CAMPFIRES

101

FOOD ON A STICK
Children love the challenge of cooking over a fire

Cooking food over a fire can be a lot of fun, even more so when you cook it on a stick. Cooking on skewers means you won't have any pots and pans to clean up. Plus, it gives a sense of accomplishment and independence from stove and cookware.

The kind of stick you use is very important. Skewers made from dead wood will simply catch fire. Wooden skewers need

to be cut from live, green saplings or branches. But since we don't advocate cutting live trees, we recommend metal or bamboo skewers that can be purchased in any grocery store.

Skewers that you are going to hold while cooking need to be at least two feet long so you can stand far enough away. If you're going to place the skewers on a metal grate, they can

Twist Bread

Shish Kebabs

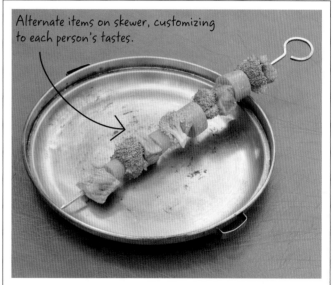

Alternate items on skewer, customizing to each person's tastes.

- Make a simple bread dough and divide into balls about the size of golf balls.

- Roll between the hands to form a rope about 8 inches long.

- Wrap dough around a stick. Hold it over red hot coals, turning frequently to bake evenly.

- Native Americans used this method, and called it bannock.

- Chop chicken or beef, firm tofu, pineapple, and vegetables like broccoli, onions, or peppers into bite-sized pieces.

- You can use things like shrimp, small bay scallops, cherry tomatoes, pearl onions, or whole mushrooms.

- Cook on a metal grate for 15 to 20 minutes, turning at least once.

- Be sure chicken and pork are completely done in the middle.

be shorter. Just be sure to use tongs to remove them.

Consider using pre-cooked meats or par-boil them to account for uneven cooking temperatures of a fire.

Hot Dogs

- Even the youngest children can put a pre-cooked hot dog on a stick, though you'll want to help them hold it over the fire.

- Slip them in a bun and top with condiments.

- For variety, wrap uncooked biscuit dough around the hot dog and cook until golden brown.

- Wrap a slice of cheese around the dog, then wrap with dough to make a cheesy dog.

S'mores

- Toast marshmallows on a skewer until browned, but not black.

- Place a chocolate bar on a graham cracker.

- Place the hot marshmallows, still on the skewer, onto the chocolate.

- Top with another graham cracker and slide out the skewer.

CAMPFIRES

FIRE'S END
Ending a fire safely is more important than building one

Natural wildfires are considered part of the natural ecosystem, renewing the forest health and maintaining biodiversity. But it's estimated that two-thirds of wildfires are started accidentally by people.

Natural fires in wilderness areas are often left to burn themselves out, but when they are too close to humans and property they need to be contained. That costs many lives and more than a billion dollars a year to fight.

Fringe areas between forest and civilization are the most at risk, and they tend to be where campgrounds are located.

Wildfires move with lightning speed, fueled by wind and dry timber. The health effects of smoke, the costs of lost timber and firefighting, not to mention the loss of human and animal life, are monumental. The irony is that the tiny spark

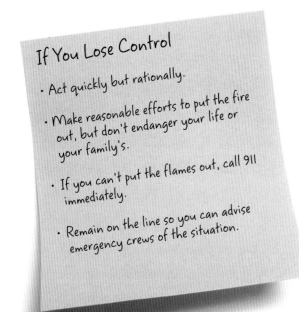

If You Lose Control

• Act quickly but rationally.

• Make reasonable efforts to put the fire out, but don't endanger your life or your family's.

• If you can't put the flames out, call 911 immediately.

• Remain on the line so you can advise emergency crews of the situation.

Burn Completely

What goes in the fire stays in the fire.

• Keep the fire small, and keep pushing unburned ends of sticks into the fire's center to burn completely.

• Never leave a fire unattended.

• Do not burn trash or leftover food.

• Stop adding wood to the fire well before bedtime so it can die down.

from a little campfire can cause such a big disaster.

Please take the time to follow the proper steps to be sure your campfire is completely out.

Douse Coals

- If possible, allow wood to burn completely to ash. Then douse it completely with water.

- Drown all embers and pour water until the hissing stops. Stir the embers with a shovel to be sure everything is wet.

- The fire must be cold to the touch. If it's too hot to touch, it's too hot to leave.

- Do not bury the fire with dirt or sand. It will continue to smolder.

Ash Disposal

- In established campgrounds, fire clean-out is usually done as part of campground maintenance.

- If not, shovel cold ashes into a trash bag and dispose.

- If you are in a primitive area, scatter the remains of ash over a large area away from camp.

- Do not bury ashes. It inhibits plant growth.

CAMPFIRES

DURABLE SURFACES
Plan ahead and prepare

Car camping shouldn't be high-impact camping. Good campers leave a place looking as they found it—or even better!

The standard policy in the outdoor world is Leave No Trace, which is both a set of ethical practices and a nonprofit organization (www.lnt.org).

The first ethic of Leave No Trace is "plan ahead and prepare." Here are some of the factors to think about and plan for be-fore you head out, from where you plan to go to having the right gear for proper food storage and disposal of waste.

How large is your group? Some areas limit group size. Consider the impact a larger group makes on the environment.

Are fires allowed? If not, you'll need to purchase a stove.

How will you handle dishwashing or unexpected bathroom breaks on a hike?

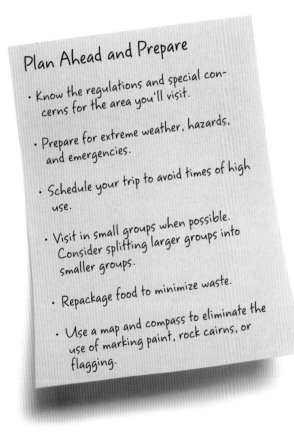

Plan Ahead and Prepare

- Know the regulations and special concerns for the area you'll visit.

- Prepare for extreme weather, hazards, and emergencies.

- Schedule your trip to avoid times of high use.

- Visit in small groups when possible. Consider splitting larger groups into smaller groups.

- Repackage food to minimize waste.

- Use a map and compass to eliminate the use of marking paint, rock cairns, or flagging.

Camp on Durable Surfaces

- Use established sites, and pitch your tent on the tent pad, if provided.

- In the absence of an obvious tent pad, try to set up where there is no vegetation.

- Do not enlarge the campsite. Altering the site is not necessary.

- Camp at least 200 feet from a lake or stream.

If you will be camping in an area of heavy bear activity, ask if it is okay to leave food in the car or if you are allowed to hang a bear bag in the campground. If neither, you'll need to purchase a bearproof canister for your food.

Here are specific practices that will make you an expert in low-impact camping to ensure that the site is ready for the next happy camper!

Travel on Durable Surfaces

- Obtain a map before you hike, and use established trails.

- Walk single file in the middle of the trail, even when it is wet or muddy.

- Be sure everyone in your group knows the importance of staying on the trail.

- Do not go off-trail, go bushwhacking, or take shortcuts up or down switchbacks, which can lead to erosion.

Pristine Areas

- Different Leave No Trace practices apply in pristine areas where there is little evidence of human impact.

- Avoid creating trails: Hike spread out with no one stepping where another has stepped.

- If camping in an area without established sites, disperse use to prevent creation of sites.

- Know ahead the practices for proper disposal of human waste and gray water and for building fires.

ZERO IMPACT

DISPOSING OF WASTE
If you pack it in, pack it out

It makes us so sad to come upon a campsite littered with food waste and a fire ring full of beer bottles. If people can carry these items into the woods, they can certainly carry them out. Like a lot of campers, we usually leave with more trash than we create.

But in addition to visible litter, there are other ways that humans impact the natural environment and make things less pleasant for the next visitor.

Washing dishes under a spigot or tossing food waste into the woods seems harmless enough. The animals will eat the food, right? Right. And they could get sick or become a nuisance to campers.

Dispose of Waste Properly

Human Waste

Use a garden or backpackers trowel to dig a cathole.

- Reduce excess food packaging and individual beverage containers at home.

- Plan on taking home your recyclables because the campground may not have receptacles.

- Inspect your campsite and rest areas for trash or spilled foods.

- Dispose of all trash, leftover food, and litter. In the absence of receptacles, or if primitive camping, take it all home.

- For day hiking, plan and explain to everyone how to handle unexpected bathroom breaks in the woods.

- It's okay to urinate in the woods; just go at least 200 feet off the trail.

- For solid human waste, dig a cathole 6 to 8 inches deep at least 200 feet from water, camp, and trails. Cover and disguise the cathole when finished. Pack out toilet paper and hygiene products in a zip-top bag.

- If you can't wash your hands with soap and water, use hand sanitizer.

Most of the time car campers will have access to a bathroom or outhouse. But occasionally nature's call comes when you're on the trail. Going to the bathroom in the woods presents a challenge, but fortunately there are accepted practices that will minimize the effect on the environment.

Dispose of food particles in the trash.

Kitchen Clean-up

- If the campground has a tub sink, use it. If not, do not wash under a spigot or in a stream or lake.

- Heat water on the stove, and pour it into a dishpan with some biodegradable soap.

- Rinse in clean water, and either towel dry or allow to air dry on the picnic table or in mesh ditty bags.

- Take the dirty dishwater to the bathhouse and dump it down the toilet.

Wash Water

- If primitive camping where there are no sinks or toilets, don't simply throw the water out in the woods or bury it. It will attract animals.

- You must first remove food particles by pouring the water through a strainer, catching the gray water in another container.

- Broadcast the gray water by flinging the pot or tub so that it spreads out over a large area.

- Broadcast strained gray water at least 200 feet from your campsite.

ZERO IMPACT

RESPECT WILDLIFE
Quietly observe from afar

As tempting as it is to get closer to that bald eagle's nest or that herd of elk, we need to observe wildlife from afar. Use binoculars or, better yet, document the sighting using a camera with a zoom lens.

Teach children early on to observe through quiet observation and to never approach, try to touch, or feed wildlife. This goes for critters large and small, no matter how cute that chipmunk gathering crumbs in the campsite.

In general, if a bird looks your way, you're too close. Do not flush birds from their nests, which can leave their eggs or young exposed to predators. Large birds like eagles, osprey, and great blue heron expend large amounts of energy when they have to fly unexpectedly.

Be sure to critterproof your campsite (see pages 78–79) to

Wildlife Checklist
- *Observe from a distance.*
- *Never feed.*
- *Store food and trash securely.*
- *Control pets at all times.*
- *Avoid wildlife during sensitive times.*

Keep Your Distance

Large herd animals can be dangerous

- Do not follow or approach any animals.

- Use a scope or zoom lens camera to observe.

- Avoid flushing birds from their nests; fleeing uses vital energy and leaves eggs or young vulnerable.

- Avoid wildlife during sensitive times: mating, nesting, raising young, or winter.

avoid unintentionally attracting and feeding wildlife.

Animals who become habituated to human contact and acquaint human presence with food eventually become nuisance or even dangerous animals. If they become too aggressive they may have to be trapped and relocated or even euthanized.

Do Not Feed

- Avoid unintentional feeding by leaving food out or in the tent or by dropping crumbs.

- Always close food tubs when they are not in use, and stow them in the car trunk right after meal prep.

- Clean up the dishes right away, and put trash either in the trunk or in a Dumpster.

- Smells quickly attract animals, especially nocturnal ones.

Bearproof

- Most often food and trash are safe in your car trunk.

- To hang a bear bag, put all your food into a ditty or duffel bag, tie a rope around the top, and sling the rope over an overhanging branch or from a metal hook provided in some campsites.

- Specially made canisters are impervious to even the most dexterous animals.

- In grizzly country, it's recommended you change the clothes you cook in and not bring them into the tent for fear the odor will attract bears.

ZERO IMPACT

111

LEAVE WHAT YOU FIND
Respect natural, historical, and cultural settings

Coming upon a rare blooming orchid, an Indian lithic field, or an intricate stone wall built by pioneer hands is an exciting find. The temptation is to take things home as treasured souvenirs. But that only spoils the sense of discovery for those who come after you.

The woods of the Appalachians where we hike are full of old stone walls, painstakingly erected by farmers in centuries past to create pastures for their cattle. Hike around these when possible. If the trail goes right over, very carefully step across without dislodging the stones.

In Florida and other coastal states, Indian middens are common. These high spots are discarded shells from centuries of seafood feasting. Never dig into these middens. If artifacts are found, leave them be.

Leave It Be

- Examine, but do not touch, cultural or historic structures and artifacts.

- Leave rocks, plants, and other natural objects as you find them. Take souvenirs in the form of photos.

- Avoid introducing or transporting non-native species.

- Do not build structures or furniture or dig trenches.

Artifacts

Never disturb or take Native American artifacts. It's illegal and many believe it brings bad luck.

- Preserve the past for others: Examine but do not touch cultural or historic structures and artifacts.

- Cultural artifacts on public land are protected by the Archaeological Resources Protection Act.

- Do not disturb pasture fencing and farmhouse ruins.

- Be content with taking photos to record and remember your find.

Even sea shelling should be limited to a few items. Old shells become homes for animals like hermit crabs. Don't fill a whole bag; take one or two representative specimens.

Respect the Earth itself. Don't dig trenches or holes or create fire rings or furniture out of trees. Tread lightly.

Antlers, fossils, even rocks are protected in national parks.

Leave Natural Features

Invasive Species

- Leave rocks, plants, and other natural objects as you find them.

- Do not move rocks, dig up soil, or go off the trail.

- Never cut trees, pound nails into trees, carve on trees, or scratch graffiti on rock walls.

- Do not pick flowers or plants, except for the occasional edible if they are abundant.

- Nonnative invasives spread quickly, outcompeting indigenous plants and literally taking over, sometimes to the point of extinction of other species.

- Examples include honeysuckle and rosa flora, but don't let their sweet-smelling beauty fool you.

- Avoid transporting and introducing invasives to other areas.

- Clean your clothes, tent, and gear before packing up camp.

ZERO IMPACT

113

MINIMIZE CAMPFIRE IMPACTS
The first question to ask yourself is whether to even build a fire

It's an enjoyable, time-honored camping tradition, but fire does impact the environment. Wood-gathering can deplete downed and decaying wood, which is a habitat for many creatures. Needless to say, an out of control fire can wreck havoc on the landscape, on human life and property.

Make an evening around the fire a treat, not something you do every night. If it's windy, or fires are prohibited, absolutely

do not build one. Today's portable stoves make it unnecessary to cook over a fire, yet doing so once in awhile can be an occasion.

Knowing how to build a low-impact fire can be a life-saver, if you're out in the backcountry, and someone is getting hypothermic. See page 97 for details on building a mound fire. All fires should be contained in a fire ring of rock or metal,

Keep Fires Small

Keep an eye on any sparks that fly away.

- Use wood no larger around than an adult wrist.

- Keep a fire burning only for the time you are using it.

- Stop adding wood well before bedtime so you can be sure everything burns.

- Do not pile large logs, or long limbs that extend past the fire ring.

Firewood

- Never cut or saw live trees.

- Use only downed and dead wood.

- Gather wood only from the ground.

- Even standing dead trees are homes for animals like pileated woodpeckers and small mammals.

in a barbecue, or a portable fire pan or grill. Only use dead and downed wood. Consider buying a bundle at the campground store so you don't have to search for, and deplete the natural supply. Most importantly, be sure there are no seasonal fire restrictions and practice fire safety.

Douse Completely

- Allow wood to burn completely to ash.

- Pour water over all embers until the hissing stops. Stir the embers with a shovel or stick to be sure everything is wet.

- It must be cold to the touch. If it's too hot to touch, it's too hot to leave.

- Do not bury the fire with dirt or sand. It will continue to smolder.

Fire Alternatives

- Use a camp stove for most of your cooking.

- A propane or battery-operated lantern creates light with the turn of a knob.

- A charcoal grill gives you the smoky taste of cooking over a fire without the hassle.

- Light some citronella candles and place them in the fire ring to give the sense of a fire, especially on a hot night.

ZERO IMPACT

CAMP ETIQUETTE

Respect other visitors and protect the quality of their outdoor experience

One of the worst night's sleep we've ever had was ironically in the middle of a wild and vast national forest.

A hard-partying group of campers was blasting heavy metal music. The campground host was no where to be found. When we finally got up the nerve to go over, sometime around two in the morning, we found that the campers had all passed out in their tents with the music on! We simply switched it off and went back to bed.

The message is this: Most people go to the woods to find solitude, enjoy nature, or escape the stresses of modern life. A little dinner music is nice, but keep the volume down, or use headphones, or enjoy nature's sounds instead. Loud voices re-

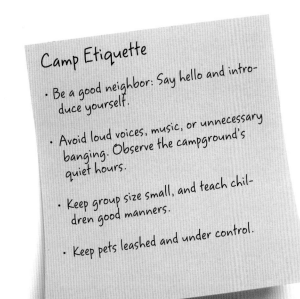

Camp Etiquette

- Be a good neighbor: Say hello and introduce yourself.

- Avoid loud voices, music, or unnecessary banging. Observe the campground's quiet hours.

- Keep group size small, and teach children good manners.

- Keep pets leashed and under control.

Respect Boundaries

- Respect the boundaries of others' campsites, and do not walk through them.

- Choose a site with natural buffers of trees, bushes, or large rocks.

- Don't make your site an eyesore by hanging laundry and leaving gear and toys scattered around.

- Observe the posted speed limit, and instruct children to bike only on campground roads.

ally carry in the outdoors: Observe the campground's posted quiet hours.

There are other aspects to respecting others' outdoor space. Keep children and pets supervised and under control. Respect the boundaries of others' campsites, and yield to others on the trail.

Maintain a buffer between groups.

Keep pets under control at all times.

Yield on Trails

- Step to the downhill side of the trail when encountering backpackers or uphill hikers. Let faster hikers pass you.

- Take breaks off the trail: Do not block the trail when stopping for a break.

- Stay in control when mountain biking. Before passing others, politely announce your presence and proceed with caution.

- Yield to those on horseback and speak quietly so as not to spook the animal. Ask first before attempting to pet a horse.

Control Pets

- You love your dog, but not everyone does!

- A dog running free can be frightening to others, and a barking dog is a real nuisance.

- Pick up dog feces from camps and trails.

- Check the regulations before you go: Some areas prohibit dogs or require them to be on a leash at all times.

ZERO IMPACT

DANGEROUS WEATHER
Hope for the best; plan for the worst

The best way to handle dangerous weather is to avoid it. Check up-to-date weather reports, listen to NOAA weather radio, or check local radar online.

Of course, sometimes that's just not possible. Summer thunderstorms and tornadoes can materialize in minutes.

If it's summer thunderstorm season, hike early in the day. They tend to develop in the afternoon. The very worst place to be is above the tree line or on an exposed ridge when the thunderstorm develops over you.

Do take lightning seriously. Approximately seventy Americans are killed each year by lightning strikes, and hundreds are injured. Most strikes occur while people are outside doing recreational activities, like hiking and camping.

The good news is that lightning strikes can be avoided with

Lightning

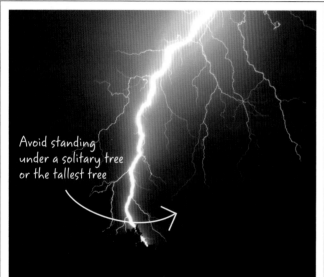

Avoid standing under a solitary tree or the tallest tree

- At the first sound of thunder, get off the water or descend from high ground immediately.

- If you are in the tent, you must get up: your tent poles are metal.

- Take shelter in a sturdy building. If you can't, get inside a metal-roofed vehicle, being careful not to touch metal inside.

- If there is no shelter, find a grove of low trees or shrubs of roughly the same height. If you are on mineral (sandy) soil, that's best. Stay there until twenty minutes after lightning is heard.

Assume the Position

- If there are no trees, find a ravine or other low spot.

- Squat down as low as possible, balancing on the balls of your feet.

- If you cannot hold this position, sit with your knees drawn up.

- Sit on a mattress pad if available to insulate you from the ground.

a few simple precautions.

Tropical storms and hurricanes, on the other hand, move slowly and with plenty of warning from the media. If you are in a coastal area during hurricane season, roughly June through October, keep an eye on the news. And do heed the warnings if a storm is coming.

Light travels faster than sound. By counting the seconds between the lightning strike and the thunder boom, you can tell how far away the storm is and whether it's moving closer or moving away. Here's how: After you see the lightning, start counting one-one-thousand, two-one-thousand, three . . . until you hear the thunder. Divide the number by five to get the miles distant: Five seconds equals 1 mile away. If the time is increasing, the storm is moving away. If it's decreasing, seek shelter immediately. For more information, visit www.lightning safety.com.

Hurricanes

- Hurricanes rarely arrive unannounced. In hurricane season, watch the weather and bring a weather radio.

- Stay away from areas likely to flash flood.

- Have an emergency route and plan in case you need to evacuate.

- Because you're camping, you'll certainly have all the supplies you'll need!

Tornadoes

A tornado watch means the conditions are favorable for formation. A tornado warning means a tornado has been spotted.

- Tornadoes develop quickly and move quite unpredictably.

- If you see the telltale funnel or a spit of dark cloud dangling from a larger one, take shelter immediately.

- During a tornado watch, you should monitor the situation closely on the radio. During a warning, leave the area the tornado is headed toward and seek shelter.

- If there is no shelter, get into a cave, ravine, or ditch. Do not get into a vehicle because it can be picked up by a tornado.

119

PREPARING FOR HEAT & COLD
How to prevent illness due to heat or cold

Be prepared and pay attention to the warning signs of hypothermia, frostbite, dehydration, or heatstroke.

First, realize that these illnesses can occur without conditions of extreme heat or cold. Hypothermia, for instance, isn't just a winter danger. It can easily strike on a hot day when a drenching rain soaks an unprepared, sweaty hiker.

On day hikes, have a bag of tricks in your backpack commensurate with the conditions: water, sports drinks, hats, bandannas, and sunscreen on hot days; extra hats, gloves, layers, high-energy snacks, and emergency blanket on cold days.

Know the weather forecast to be prepared for a storm or a drop in temperature. Have appropriate layers for wind, rain, and cold for everyone in the group, and encourage their use.

Remove or add layers according to activity level, temperature, and weather.

Preventing Hypothermia and Frostbite

- Dress in layers appropriate to conditions.

- Bring warm hat and gloves, extra socks, rain gear, and an emergency blanket.

- Nibble high-energy foods.

- Keep hydrated.

- Don't ignore the warning signs: uncontrollable shivering, clumsiness, slurred speech for hypothermia; numbness or prickling pain for frostbite.

Layering

- Dress in layers to control body temperature and avoid sweating (see Chapter 4 for details).

- The base layer should be a long-sleeved top and long bottoms of synthetic or a synthetic/wool blend, never cotton.

- Put on a windproof layer at the top of a peak.

- Have waterproof rain gear in case of rain or snow.

Pay special attention to children whose small bodies and higher metabolisms are more sensitive to extremes than those of adults.

It's not enough to ask, "Are you thirsty?" By the time they feel thirst, mild dehydration has already set in. Encourage frequent water breaks whether or not they feel thirsty.

GREEN ● LIGHT

Sun protection: Avoid sunburn, wrinkles, and future skin cancers by using a high-SPF broad-spectrum sunscreen, preferably one that contains a physical barrier as well, like zinc oxide or a variation. Avoid direct sun exposure from 11 A.M. to 3 P.M., and wear lightweight, light-colored clothing to cover up. Don't forget sunglasses, a hat, and plenty of water.

Add sports drink powder to water to make it more enticing to kids.

Stay Hydrated

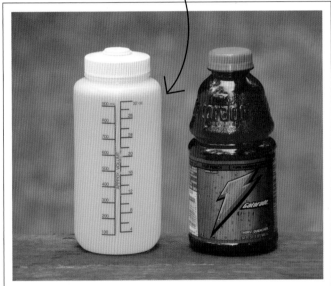

- During physical activity, it's important to stay hydrated in cold and hot, humid weather.

- Drink before, during, and after strenuous activity, especially in humid weather, but also in cold weather, which depresses the body's natural thirst mechanism.

- Drink water at every rest stop, but don't gulp: The body can better absorb several small mouthfuls.

- Sports drinks replenish electrolytes lost through sweating, but beware of too much sugar.

Preventing Heat Illness

- Try to do strenuous activities during cooler times of the day, like early morning or evening.

- Take frequent water breaks and try to stay in the shade.

- If you feel overheated, dip a bandanna in a stream and put it around your head, or dip your shirt and let it dry on your back.

- Keep a close eye on the kids: Children overheat more easily than adults.

WATER SAFETY
Take care on the beach or in the boat

A fair number of camping vacations are held near the water, whether it's an ocean or a mountain lake. Like bees to honey, if there's water nearby, kids will find it to take a cooling swim or just to skip rocks.

Learn about the water sources near your camp, and instruct children not to go near them without letting you know. They should never swim without adult supervision.

Practice safe boating by first knowing your vessel. Do not rent a powerboat if you've never driven one. If you keep canoes or kayaks near the water, store the paddles somewhere else so children aren't tempted to take them out without you.

Everyone in a boat needs a Coast Guard-approved life jacket aboard, and children twelve and under should always have theirs on and buckled.

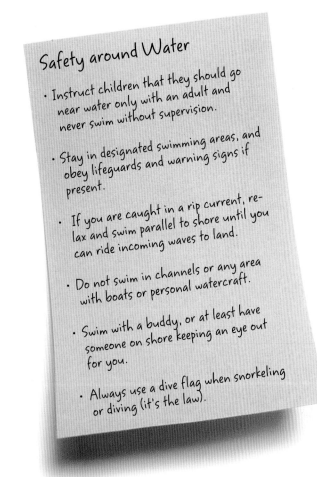

Safety around Water

- Instruct children that they should go near water only with an adult and never swim without supervision.

- Stay in designated swimming areas, and obey lifeguards and warning signs if present.

- If you are caught in a rip current, relax and swim parallel to shore until you can ride incoming waves to land.

- Do not swim in channels or any area with boats or personal watercraft.

- Swim with a buddy, or at least have someone on shore keeping an eye out for you.

- Always use a dive flag when snorkeling or diving (it's the law).

Life Jackets

Be sure the jacket is snug, or else it will simply float above the head if submerged

- When boating, children should always wear a Coast Guard-approved life jacket.

- Everyone on board should have one readily accessible. It's the law, and failing to do so can get you a hefty fine.

- Life jackets should fit snugly with two or three straps around the torso.

- Check the weight recommendation on the label to be sure everyone has access to an appropriate jacket.

Shark attacks get a lot of attention, and, yes, they can be terrifying and deadly. But the chances of drowning or being in a boat accident are exponentially greater. Take care: Don't be a statistic.

ZOOM

Tips for avoiding sharks:
1. Do not swim at feeding time: twilight or after dark. 2. Don't wear shiny jewelry or metallic bathing suits. 3. Don't swim if you are bleeding from a wound or menstruating. 4. Don't go too far from shore, and swim in groups. 5. Avoid sharp dropoffs and areas off sandbars, which are favorite hang-outs for sharks.

At the Beach

- Obey the colored flag or sign if posted on the beach.

- Red means to avoid any water contact.

- Yellow cautions of strong currents, rip tides, or rough water.

- Green means go for a swim.

Lifeguards

- If anyone is an unsure swimmer, or if you have small children, seek out a lifeguarded beach.

- Be sure to obey the lifeguard's warnings and whistle blasts if you get too far out.

- If there is a designated swimming area, stay inside it.

- Do not swim in areas with boats or personal watercraft.

BOTHERSOME PLANTS
Don't let pesky plants spoil your vacation

Instruct children to never eat berries unless you approve them first. And mushrooms should be off-limits to all but the aficionado.

Some stinging plants are just a nuisance, but an entire trip can be ruined by a bad case of poison ivy. Teach the kids how to identify it in its various incarnations.

The three-leafed enemy, along with poison oak, poison sumac, and the poisonwood tree, produces an annoying red, itchy rash and fluid-filled bumps.

Wear long pants when hiking on trails where poison ivy is present or in tall grass where nettles might be. It's a myth that poison ivy rash is spread by itching or being in contact with others. It comes from being in direct contact with the oil of the plant.

Stinging Nettles

The hairs become needles, injecting a cocktail of irritants into the skin.

- The leaves are easy to identify: The edges are hairy and serrated.

- Wear long pants and avoid brushing against this plant, which can reach chest high.

- Apply a cold compress and anti-itch cream to the sting.

- Nettles actually have medicinal uses, and when cooked taste like spinach, but we haven't gotten up the nerve to try!

Poison Ivy

The adage "Leaves of three, let it be" still holds true

- Poison ivy and poison oak have several varieties, but all have clusters of three leaflets.

- It can be a low ground cover, a shrub, or a vine climbing a tree. Leaves can be green or red.

- Check your campsite and nearby area, and instruct everyone on identification.

- If contact is made, wash skin with soap and cold water immediately.

Reaction varies greatly among different people. Some can simply walk by a plant, and their eyes swell up, whereas others seem to be immune. If you are in the former category, carry medication with you and take care to avoid the plant.

Berries

- White berries are almost always poisonous. Red holly berries are as well.

- If such berries are accidentally eaten, drink water and induce vomiting. If a large amount is consumed or if you get sick, seek medical attention.

- But raspberries, blueberries, and blackberries are easy to identify in the wild. They're usually smaller versions of their grocery store counterparts. If in doubt, don't try it.

- Gather them up, rinse with cold water, and put them on cereal or in a fruit cobbler.

Mushrooms

- There are numerous poisonous mushrooms that look like their edible counterparts.

- Results of eating them range from a stomachache to death.

- In case of ingestion of an unknown kind, take the person and a sample of the mushroom to a medical facility.

- Edible morels and ink caps are easy to identify, but if you are at all in doubt, don't risk it.

DANGEROUS INSECTS
Avoid these biting, stinging critters while out on the trail

Mosquitoes can ruin a good time, whereas other biting insects can be downright dangerous.

Bee, wasp, and even scorpion stings are painful but normally not serious. Tick bites, on the other hand, can lead to serious chronic illness.

Lyme disease and Rocky Mountain Spotted Fever are bacterial infections spread to humans (and animals, including dogs) by the bite of an infected tick.

Both are found throughout the U.S. and can be effectively treated early on with antibiotics. If left untreated, Lyme disease can become chronic and quite debilitating, and Rocky Mountain Spotted Fever can be fatal.

Lyme disease is transmitted by the bite of infected deer ticks, which are black and often no larger than a pinhead.

Ticks

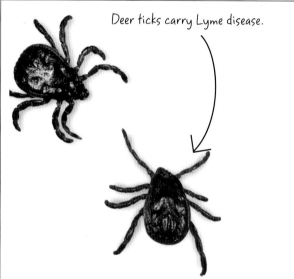

Deer ticks carry Lyme disease.

- Conduct tick checks every night: Take off your clothes and check, particularly the groin, armpits, neck, and scalp. Ticks like dark, hairy places. Check the kids and the dog, too.

- Removal: Use tweezers to gently pull a tick out in the direction it went in. Be careful that the head doesn't come off in your skin.

- Treatment: Wash and wipe with antiseptic. Keep an eye on the bite.

- If flulike symptoms or a bull's-eye rash develops, see a doctor soon for a round of antibiotics.

Bees and Wasps

Use a needle or tweezers to remove the stinger if left in the skin.

- These stings can be painful, but symptoms usually subside in a few hours.

- Treatment: Wash the sting and wipe with antiseptic. Use a needle or tweezers to remove the stinger if left. Take an antihistamine if itching or swelling is uncomfortable.

- If a severe allergic reaction occurs, such as difficulty breathing, seek emergency care immediately.

- If you know you are allergic, always carry antihistamine and a hypodermic kit if instructed by your doctor.

Just because you find an embedded tick doesn't mean you'll automatically get sick. First of all, not all types of ticks carry disease. Second, research shows that early removal of the tick, within thirty-six hours, greatly reduces the chances of transmittal. So don't panic.

Early signs include flulike symptoms, fatigue, and a telltale bull's-eye rash around the bite. See a doctor immediately if these occur.

ZOOM

Avoiding ticks: They like tall grass and warm weather. When hiking in tick season, spray shoes and lower legs with bug spray. Wear closed-toed shoes and socks and long, light-colored pants so you can see any that crawl up your legs, and brush them off. Dogs should be on flea and tick prevention and should get a tick check before coming inside the tent or home.

Spiders

- Spider bites are usually nothing to worry about, with two exceptions:

- The brown recluse has a violin shape on its back. The bite produces a bull's-eye around a blister and can lead to a variety of medical problems. See a doctor if this occurs.

- The black widow is shiny with an hourglass shape. Severe muscle cramping, fever, chills, and nausea may occur.

- For these types of bites, medical attention is usually recommended, especially for children and the elderly.

Scorpions

- There are many types of scorpions in the U.S., but only the centruroides, found in the Southwest, are truly dangerous.

- If you are stung, wash the area with soap and water and apply antiseptic. An oral antihistamine can help with swelling.

- Apply a cool compress or ice wrapped in a cloth for ten-minute intervals.

- If convulsions, impaired vision or speech, nausea, vomiting, difficult breathing, or impaired circulation occur, go to a hospital for an antivenin.

127

DANGEROUS ANIMALS
Keep your distance from wildlife, and they will keep their distance from you

With a few exceptions, nearly all wild animals you'll encounter in North America would just as soon avoid you.

However, animals who become habituated to human contact soon acquaint human presence with food. (Thus, it's important to properly stow away all food [see page 78].) These animals eventually become a nuisance or even dangerous.

If they become too aggressive they may have to be trapped and relocated or even euthanized.

Even if an animal is not aggressive, accidental encounters can take place, from stepping on a snake to startling a bear in the woods. A frightened animal is a dangerous one.

Like most wild animals, mountain lions, alligators, and bear

Poisonous Snakes

In general, venomous snakes have patterns.

- Venomous snakes are common throughout the U.S. and include rattlesnakes and coral snakes, which live on land, and cottonmouths (water moccasins) and copperheads, which can be in the water.

- Avoid all snakes.

- Be cautious when hiking on rocks, especially warmed by the sun, a favorite hang-out for rattlers.

- Stay on the trail and avoid walking through tall grass.

Black Bear

- Black bears are common throughout the U.S., but dangerous encounters are rare. Black bears mostly just want your garbage!

- The grizzly bear, found only in the northwest U.S. and Canada, is much larger and far more aggressive.

- When hiking in bear country, stay on trails and make noise. Some hikers wear a jingly bell on their pack or walking stick.

- It's imperative to keep an immaculate campsite in bear country. Even lip balm and toothpaste can attract bears.

have a natural fear of humans. However, encounters have increased as human population centers expand into previously wild territory.

Thousands of venomous snake bites are reported each year, but only a handful are fatal.

The best course is to avoid animals and to be sure to critter-proof your campsite (see pages 78–79) to avoid unintentionally attracting and feeding wildlife.

YELLOW ● LIGHT

Beware of any animal that seems over–friendly. Boldness in a wild animal can be a sign of rabies. Particularly be wary of nocturnal animals like raccoons wandering around in the sun, another sign they might be carrying the disease. Be sure your pet's vaccinations are up-to-date.

Alligator

- Alligator attacks can certainly be lethal. A handful of human and pet deaths occur in Florida each year.

- In the wild, alligators shy away from humans. However, in populated areas, they can become a danger to humans and pets.

- Always keep your distance, and be aware of the potential of alligator presence when swimming.

- If you see an alligator posing a threat, contact authorities. Do not try to divert it to another area or kill it.

Mountain Lion

It is also known as "cougar," "panther," or "puma."

- Mountain lions live in the western U.S., particularly in California, where they can exist anywhere there are deer for prey.

- Never hike alone in mountain lion territory. Go in groups, keep children close, and make noise to scare away mountain lions.

- Never run away from a mountain lion; doing so stimulates the natural instinct to chase.

- If you encounter one that does not run away, make noise, and flap your arms to make yourself look larger (and less like prey!).

FIRST AID KIT
Be prepared with a good, stocked kit

A good first aid kit is a necessity on a camping trip. First aid kits can be purchased in numerous sizes, from a tiny pocket pouch for minor wounds to a full-fledged wilderness medical kit that could save someone's life.

Choose a kit based on the size of your group, the ages of the group's members, their medical condition, how active they are, and how far away from help you tend to go. From there you will customize it, adding some medications or items based on your group's medical condition or history.

Familiarize yourself with items in the kit and their purpose: They're no good if you don't know how to use them. When packing your kit, remember that see-through zippered pouches allow you to locate items quickly. To save space, fill tiny zip-top baggies from larger bottles.

Basic Kit

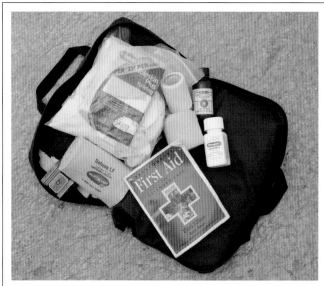

- At the least you need gauze to stop bleeding, bandages in various sizes, latex gloves, scissors, antiseptic, antibiotic ointment, tweezers, and so forth.

- Other items might include a digital thermometer, instant hot or cold pack, moleskin for blisters, sting and itch relief, and basic over-the-counter medications.

- Purchase a small kit to take day hiking, a larger one to keep at camp or in the car.

- The kit should have a first aid instruction guide.

Deluxe Kit

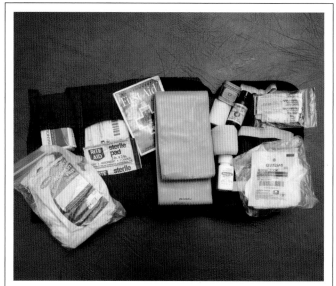

- An adventure or wilderness first aid kit is advisable if you will be far from medical help.

- The idea is that you will be able to stabilize a serious illness or injury until help can arrive.

- The kit should have every-thing the basic kit has but in larger quantities.

- Additionally it should have CPR mouth guard, splints, Ace bandages, disposable syringe for irrigating wounds, medical tape, rolls of gauze, sterile wound dressings, and an emergency blanket.

A good first aid kit should be considered a work in progress. On nearly every trip, you'll undoubtedly wish for some item that's not in there: Make a note to add that item when you get home.

Before the next trip you should restock anything that was used and check medications for expiration dates or damage due to heat or moisture.

····· **GREEN ● LIGHT** ·····

Consider taking the Red Cross's first aid and CPR course, particularly if you have children. Just a few hours of your time will give you the confidence to handle basic first aid and could even save someone's life.

Medications

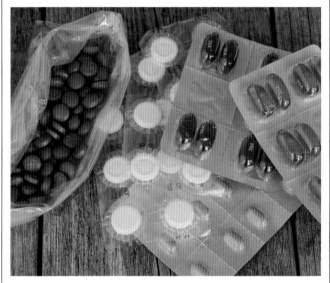

- Over-the-counter must-haves: Ibuprofen, antihistamine, anti-nausea, anti-diarrhea, antacid, and cold medicine.

- Be sure to bring any medications that have been prescribed by a physician.

- Vitamins: multi-vitamin, vitamin C, and Echinacea in case anyone feels like he or she is coming down with a cold.

- If you have kids, consider children's chewable or liquid versions.

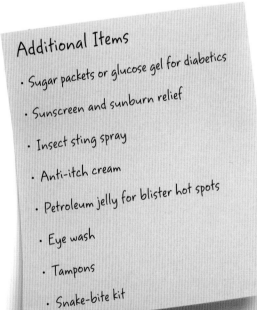

Additional Items
- Sugar packets or glucose gel for diabetics
- Sunscreen and sunburn relief
- Insect sting spray
- Anti-itch cream
- Petroleum jelly for blister hot spots
- Eye wash
- Tampons
- Snake-bite kit

WOUNDS, BURNS, & BLISTERS
Take care of minor ailments so they don't become major ones

This chapter is not intended to take the place of a first aid course or even a good first aid manual: You should really get both if you are going to be in the outdoors with your family.

Presented here are the basics for how to take care of minor injuries and how to identify and initially treat the major ones until you can get help.

Blisters, cuts, and abrasions are going to be the most com-

mon problem—and hopefully your worst! So, especially with children, you'll be restocking the Band-Aids and antiseptic quite often.

Even the smallest breaks in the skins should be treated to prevent infection and reduce pain.

You should have a plan in case something more serious occurs. Where is the nearest hospital? Do you have a vehi-

When to Get Help

- If a wound will not close and stitches are required.

- Severe burns

- Severe bleeding

- Bone fractures

- Loss of consciousness

Blisters

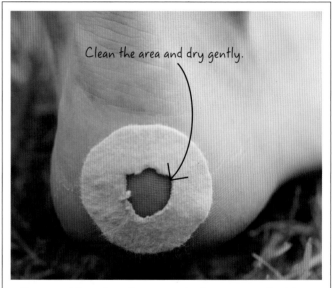

Clean the area and dry gently.

- Prevent a blister from forming by applying petroleum jelly to hot spots.

- After a blister has formed, do not pop it unless you need to keep hiking.

- In that case, pop it with a sterile needle and apply antibiotic ointment.

- Apply a clean bandage, padded moleskin, or gel-like dressings that cushion the skin.

cle? Does your cell phone have a strong signal in the campground? If not, is the campground phone accessible twenty-four hours?

If anyone in your group is extremely old or young or has any pre-existing conditions, even minor injuries should be taken seriously.

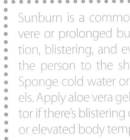
ZOOM

Sunburn is a common outdoor ailment, but severe or prolonged burning can lead to dehydration, blistering, and eventually skin cancer. Move the person to the shade and give water to sip. Sponge cold water on the skin or apply wet towels. Apply aloe vera gel or other remedy. See a doctor if there's blistering over a large part of the body or elevated body temperature.

Minor Wounds

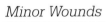

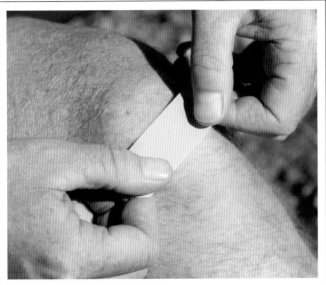

- Clean and cover even small breaks in the skin to prevent infection.

- Cool minor burns with water until the pain is gone.

- Clean wounds with water and dry thoroughly.

- Apply antibiotic ointment and bandage with an appropriately sized dressing.

Serious Bleeding

Wear latex gloves to prevent infection.

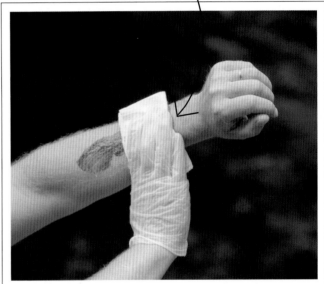

- To slow bleeding, apply pressure with gauze pads, pushing the edges of the wound together.

- If possible, hold the wound higher than the patient's heart.

- Do not attempt to use a tourniquet or suture the wound.

- Get medical help as soon as possible.

BITES & STINGS

These kinds of injuries are usually minor but can be life threatening

In most cases, insect bites and stings are a temporary discomfort. However, if someone is highly allergic, he or she can go into anaphylactic shock, a rapidly progressing condition that can cause death.

Whenever a person is stung by a bee, always ask if he or she has had prior bad reactions. They usually get progressively worse each time. If the person carries a hypodermic kit, help the person administer it immediately.

Ticks can carry Lyme disease and Rocky Mountain Spotted Fever, so do regular tick checks of yourself, children, and dogs.

Just because you find an embedded tick doesn't mean you'll automatically get sick. Early signs include flulike symptoms, fatigue, and a telltale bull's-eye rash around the bite. See a doctor immediately if this happens.

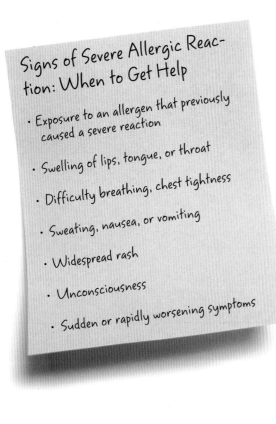

Signs of Severe Allergic Reaction: When to Get Help

- Exposure to an allergen that previously caused a severe reaction

- Swelling of lips, tongue, or throat

- Difficulty breathing, chest tightness

- Sweating, nausea, or vomiting

- Widespread rash

- Unconsciousness

- Sudden or rapidly worsening symptoms

Proper Tick Removal

- Use tweezers to gently pull a tick out in the direction it went in. Be careful that the head doesn't come off in your skin.

- Wash and wipe with antiseptic.

- If flu-like symptoms or a bull's-eye rash develops, see a doctor for a round of antibiotics.

- Ticks can carry Lyme disease and Rocky Mountain Spotted Fever, but tick removal within thirty-six hours greatly reduces the risk.

In the U.S. there are only two types of spiders to worry about: the brown recluse and the black widow. See a doctor if you know you've been bitten by one of them. Otherwise, keep an eye out for blistering, discoloration, muscle cramping, fever, chills, nausea, or any of the severe allergic symptoms listed below.

Insect Bites

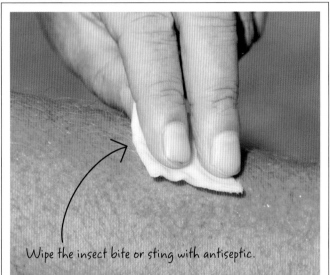

Wipe the insect bite or sting with antiseptic.

- Be sure to remove a bee's stinger with a sterilized needle.

- Relieve swelling with an ice pack and itching with a sting-relief spray or oral antihistamine.

- Get help at the first sign of respiratory distress or other sign of severe allergic reaction.

- After you've had a severe reaction, always carry a hypodermic kit to treat anaphylactic shock.

Snake Bites

In venomous snake-infested areas, you may want to carry a snake-bite kit.

- Not all snakes are poisonous, so you should know the symptoms of a venomous bite.

- Go to a hospital if any of these symptoms occur: swelling, discoloration, blistering, or severe pain around the bite; diarrhea or nausea; convulsion, dizziness, or fainting.

- Remove anything, like jewelry, that might restrict circulation.

- Gently wash the site, but do not apply cold packs or tourniquets or cut or suck the site.

SPRAINS & FRACTURES
Sometimes it's difficult to tell the difference

Whenever outdoor activity occurs, whether it's climbing a mountain or playing a game of soccer, sprains and fractures can result.

Sprains are an injury to the ligaments that can usually be treated by the RICE method: Rest, ice, compress, and elevate.

Fractures are bone breaks, which can be obvious, in the case of a compound fracture when the bone breaks through the skin, or invisible hairline fractures that can be detected only by an X-ray.

Sometimes it's difficult to tell the difference between a sprain and a fracture because both cause pain, swelling, and bruising. When in doubt, treat like a fracture to be on the safe side because moving a fractured bone can cause more damage.

Sprain or Fracture? Signs of a Fracture Include:

- Difficulty moving the limb
- Cannot bear weight
- Visible deformity
- Swelling and discoloration
- Pain persists, even after RICE treatment
- If still unsure, treat the injury as a fracture.

RICE

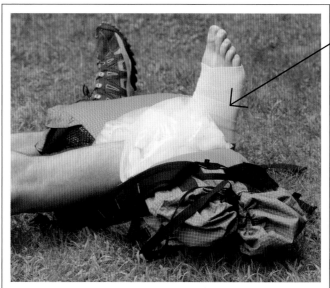

- Rest. If you are out in the woods, rest or help the person to walk out if possible.

- Ice. Use ice to reduce pain and swelling. If none is available, use a cloth soaked in cold water or snow.

- Compress. Use a gentle pressure by applying an Ace bandage.

- Elevate. If possible, raise the injury above the heart.

Don't attempt to treat a fracture. Leave it to the professionals so you don't do more harm than good.

If you are out hiking in the woods, you should first try your cell phone or send a third person for help. If you absolutely have to move a person with a fracture, immobilize the limb by making a splint or sling and provide assistance in walking.

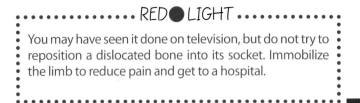
Treat sprains initially with this method.

Wrapping Sprains

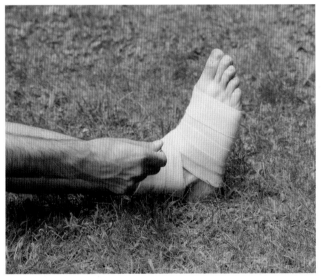

- Do not wrap so tightly as to cut off circulation.

- The elastic bandage should be applied at about half of its potential for stretching.

- Wrap a foot in a figure-8 pattern, from near the base of the toes up toward the calf.

- If a fracture is suspected, go to the hospital.

Fractures

- If you're sure you have a fracture, go to a hospital immediately or summon an ambulance.

- If you are out in the woods and cannot summon help, do your best to immobilize the limb:

- Use a sling to immobilize a broken arm or a splint on a broken leg. You can also bandage a broken leg to the sound one.

- Protect protruding bone with dressing.

137

HEAT & COLD
Identify and treat illness due to extreme temperatures

Previously we talked about *preventing* conditions like hypothermia, frostbite, dehydration, and heatstroke. Here we'll discuss how to *identify* these maladies and what initial *treatment* to give until you can get medical attention.

We are not doctors, and if you aren't either, don't try to handle a serious situation on your own. You should know how to recognize the warning signs of serious illness and how best to give initial treatment until help arrives.

Minor cases of numb fingers, mild dehydration, and borderline hypothermia may not require a trip to the emergency room. But knowing when to take that step is vital.

If the person cannot speak or loses consciousness, that's a no-brainer: Get help immediately. But even mild cases can get worse quickly, so if your treatment doesn't have an effect

Drink fluids with electrolytes.

Symptoms of Heat Illnesses

- Dehydration: thirst, nausea, headache, dizziness, cramps, fatigue, lack of urine

- Heat exhaustion: headache, fainting, confusion, damp pale skin, cramps, nausea, fast pulse

- Heatstroke: headache, dizziness, confusion, body temperature above 104, flushed hot skin, fast pulse

Treating Heat Exhaustion

- Cool the person by having the person rest in the shade.

- Place a wet towel or bandanna on face and neck.

- Heat exhaustion can lead to life-threatening heatstroke.

- Monitor body temperature and symptoms. If they do not subside, get help.

quickly, get professional help.

   If the person has a pre-existing condition like diabetes or heart or kidney disease or is extremely young or old, be safe and get medical attention.

ZOOM

Treating frostbite: If possible, go to a warm, dry shelter. Remove wet clothing. Use body heat to warm the area: Put hands under the armpits, behind the knees, or on the stomach. If the feet are affected, use another person. Do not rub because this can damage the skin. If feeling does not return soon, or if the tissue is blue or black, seek medical help to prevent permanent damage or loss of tissue.

A warm hat is the best way to prevent further heat loss.

Treating Hypothermia

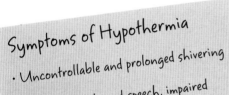

Symptoms of Hypothermia

• Uncontrollable and prolonged shivering

• Clumsiness, slurred speech, impaired judgment

• Severe: shivering stops, victim unable to move, pulse weakens

- Stop movement and seek a warm, dry shelter.

- Remove damp clothing and add layers of dry clothing.

- Give warm drinks (no alcohol) and high-energy snacks.

- Seek medical help immediately if person is unconscious or if condition does not improve.

EMERGENCIES
Know when to call for help and have an emergency plan

Certain situations require immediate medical intervention. Others can wait until you drive to an emergency room or doctor's office or even until you get home and see your own doctor.

Avoiding panic and assessing the situation quickly, but not rashly, are crucial.

Clearly if a person is not breathing, has no pulse, is bleeding severely, has a protruding bone, or is unconscious, you should call for help right away.

Shock is a potentially life-threatening condition that can sneak up on you. Shock is a failure of the circulatory system, which can be caused by severe blood loss, severe burns, fractures, heatstroke, or hypothermia. Even a person with a seemingly mild injury can slip into shock, so it's important

Handling Emergencies

- Stay calm and take charge.

- Be sure the scene is safe.

- Check for immediate threats: no breathing, no pulse, severe blood loss, unconsciousness.

- Call 911 or send for help if you can't.

- If the person is not breathing, perform CPR.

- If the person is conscious, ask her if she has any medical conditions; check for a medical alert bracelet and tell the medical personnel.

Shock

Take a pulse with two fingers on the inner wrist, just below the thumb.

- Shock can be caused by severe blood loss, severe burns, fractures, heatstroke, or hypothermia.

- Symptoms are fast, weak pulse; cool, pale skin; chills; confusion; lack of urine.

- Action: Until help arrives, keep the person warm, calm, and comfortable, lying down with legs elevated.

- Monitor the person's breathing and pulse rate, taking notes to give emergency personnel.

to monitor the victim, know the signs, and get help immediately.

Use a cell phone to call 911. If you can't get service, climb to a high point to get better reception. If you still have no service, send someone for help.

Rescue Breathing

- Take a Red Cross CPR course for training in this technique.

- If a person is unconscious but breathing, attempt to revive the person while assessing the cause.

- If the person is not breathing, clear the airway and start rescue breathing.

- Use a plastic face shield to prevent the spread of germs.

CPR

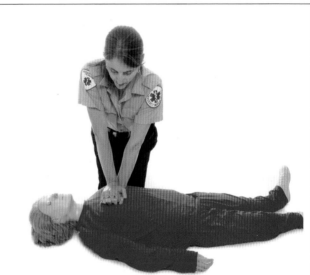

- Take a Red Cross CPR course for training.

- This technique has changed recently, so if it's been a few years, retake the course.

- If a person has no pulse and is not breathing, do a combination of rescue breathing and CPR chest compressions.

- Continue until medical help arrives.

PLANNING

Involve children in planning the trip to get them excited about the camping experience

When you involve children in planning or selecting some aspect of the trip, they'll have a sense of ownership and be more engaged.

Depending on age and interest, you can let children help choose a destination, campsite, features, or activities.

You can let the kids be very involved, such as in picking the state or park, or let them choose from a few pre-selected campgrounds. Let them look at the map and help decide which campsite to select, or simply let them plan the wish list of items on the camping itinerary.

Consider child-friendly features in choosing a destination and campground. There might be a lake with a beach or boat

Kid-friendly Nature

Hike to a reward: a view, a waterfall, or an old homestead.

- Hiking is one of the premier joys of camping. But if a trail is too long or too steep for the kids, it can turn into drudgery.

- Research the trails ahead of time, and obtain the appropriate trail maps.

- Choose trails commensurate with age and ability, and make frequent rest stops.

- Don't overlook the trails within your own campground. A loop around camp makes a nice after-dinner activity.

Waterfront

- Kids love water, so campgrounds near a lake, stream, or the ocean are big hits.

- Water opens up a myriad of things to do: swimming, boating, kayaking, fishing, or simply skipping rocks.

- Find out what types of activities are available and plan accordingly.

- Do note the water safety checklists on page 122.

ramp, a playground, ball fields, recreation room, or a swimming pond.

Work some day hikes into the itinerary, commensurate with age and ability. Let the kids help pick routes that have a reward built in: a climbable feature, a dramatic rock formation, a waterfall, a great view, or a pioneer homestead. It's hard to plan wildlife spottings, but there are places where you're more likely to see certain birds or other animals.

Campfire

Make an evening around the fire a treat.

- Although it's not necessary or prudent to have a fire every night, at least one night you should plan to sit around the fire and make s'mores.

- Be sure the campground you are going to allows fires and doesn't have a temporary ban.

- Pick up a bundle of wood and bring kindling and newspaper so there won't be any disappointment.

- Be sure to follow safe fire practices, outlined on page 98.

How to Involve Kids

- Let kids help select the location.

- Study nature/geology/history in advance for your child.

- Research activities in advance for your child.

- Create a checklist of fun things to bring: bikes, balls, bathing suits, fishing poles.

- Make a list of fun things to do and see.

INFANTS

With the right conditions, your children are never too young to start camping

We believe the outdoors can have a profound and positive effect on people of all ages.

Many people believe that it's easier to wait until a baby can sit up on its own or is around five or six months old before going camping. Others find that younger babies are extremely portable and need very little gear: clean clothes, diapers, bottles, and formula (unless you are nursing).

As long as the weather is good and there is little environmental stress, there's no reason to avoid car camping with baby. It can offer many of the comforts of home in a serene, natural setting.

Older babies and toddlers actually need more gear and su-

Baby Carrier

The sound of a parent's heartbeat is soothing to baby.

- Babies younger than three months or so can be carried in a slinglike carrier.

- This provides you with a hands-free option to do camp chores, read a book, or go for a walk.

- The comfort and closeness provided by a baby sling are good for nursing, napping, or sitting around the fire talking.

- There are many styles: Choose one that is ergonomic and won't cause back strain.

Backpack Carrier

- This is a great way to take babies and toddlers on the trail, sightseeing, or on a walk through the campground.

- Many infants fall asleep to the jostling motion.

- Be sure the child wears a hat for sun protection.

- Babies usually have to be five or six months old to sit in these carriers.

144

pervision so they don't wander off. Be sure to bring some sort of conveyance—a carrier, stroller, or tricycle—for trips around the campground or short day hikes.

Youngsters love to feel like they are helping. Older toddlers can help with camp chores like filling water jugs, stirring food (not on the stove!), setting the table, or washing dishes.

Be sure the carrier has a good hip belt to keep weight off your shoulders.

Playing

- Set up a safe place for baby to play.

- The inside of the tent on top of a cushy sleeping bag is a great place to play, read a book, or take a nap.

- Spread a blanket out on the grass with some favorite toys.

- If you have room in the car, bring a playpen for a clean, safe place to play.

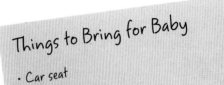

Things to Bring for Baby

- Car seat
- Food, formula
- Diaper bag
- Sling or backpack carrier
- Stroller
- Playpen
- Favorite toys and books
- Tricycle

CHILDREN & PETS

145

CHILDREN AROUND CAMP
Start you camping trip with an orientation around the grounds

Soon after choosing your campsite, walk children around the perimeter so they know how far they can go. Reiterate rules like letting you know where they are going. Sometimes they forget house rules when away from home.

Locate the bathhouse, and based on their age decide if this is a place the children can go on their own or only with you. Locate any potential hazards like water, cliffs, or roadways.

Instruct children on zero impact practices (see pages 106–115), such as picking up trash, staying on established paths, leaving plants and artifacts intact, and not damaging live trees.

Point out any poisonous plants and remind the children not to eat anything like wild mushrooms or berries.

You'll also want to point out some of the fun things you'll

Natural Toys

- A child's innate creativity and imagination kick in when outdoors.

- A collection of sticks, stones, and acorns becomes a building or town.

- A longer stick becomes a hiking staff.

- A hole in a tree becomes a place where elves or fairies might live.

Nature Study

- Bring field guides on trees, plants, and bugs to study and identify.

- Observe butterflies, caterpillars, ladybugs, and other safe insects.

- Use a fish net, butterfly net, or bug box to safely and gently collect and observe, then release.

- Identify plants and trees and their medicinal or commercial uses.

be doing during your stay: a hiking trailhead, the recreation room, or the camp store (which usually sells ice cream!).

Now it's time to head back to camp and make sure the tent is up and the kitchen is set up for dinner. Everyone can have a job to do, no matter how young. Make it fun! Learning to live outdoors is exciting.

•••••••••••••••••• RED ● LIGHT ••••••••••••••••

Instruct children on what to do if they become lost: Don't panic. Someone will be looking for you soon. Sit down and don't go wandering farther. Wear a whistle and blow it, or start yelling "help" at regular intervals.

Nighttime Fun

- Using a flashlight, make shadow puppets on the tent wall.

- Bring a star chart to identify planets and constellations.

- Go on a nighttime walk to listen for crickets, frogs, and owls.

- Catch lightning bugs in a jar.

Campground Safety Rules for Kids

- Always tell a parent where you are going.

- Never swim without adult supervision.

- What goes in the fire stays in the fire.

- Don't talk to strangers.

- Always wear a bike helmet.

FOOD & WATER

Happy tummies make happy campers, so be sure you have lots of food supplies on hand

Camp food should not be boring. Bring favorites from home for comfort, but add in some outdoor foods like GORP and silver turtles that the kids get every day.

Involve kids in the menu planning and let them go grocery shopping with you. Try innovative ways to make family favorites outdoors. Throw in some recipes for fun, like dinner on a stick. If children have a say, they'll be more likely to help with preparation and to eat the stuff!

Make mealtime a fun project, not a chore. Kids can help prep vegetables, measure, unwrap items, and stir ingredients together. Cooking over the stove should be reserved for older children.

Snacks

- Pack long-lasting, nonperishable snacks in zip-top bags or watertight containers.

- Durable fresh fruit like apples and oranges come in their own packaging.

- Other healthy snacks include dried fruit, gra-nola bars, soy chips, cheese crackers, pretzels, and muffins.

- GORP (good old raisins and peanuts) is a mainstay, even better when you add M&Ms, chocolate, or carob bits.

Be Prepared

Keep snackables in an easy-to-reach pocket.

- Even on short hikes, be sure you have enough water and snacks for everyone.

- Juice pouches or powdered energy drinks added to water bottles will encourage hydration.

- Bring a small trash bag for waste, and instruct children on the importance of not dropping crumbs for wildlife.

- Stop frequently for snack and water breaks.

Have plenty of nutritious and interesting snacks. We all burn more calories when we're outside and active.

Pay close attention to how much water and other liquids the kids (and pets, for that matter) are consuming. Children get dehydrated more quickly than adults and may not think to tell you they are thirsty.

Never sit in front of a stove. You need to move quickly in case of a spill.

Helping

- Set up stations on the picnic table for the different stages of meal prep: washing, peeling, chopping, and opening cans.

- Set out the food and required utensils. Then call over some helpers.

- Don't light the stove until you are ready so you're not distracted from it.

- Only older children should help at the stove and always under adult supervision.

Camp Meals That Kids Love

- Silver turtles

- Shish kebabs

- Dutch oven lasagna

- Blueberry pancakes

- Lunch wraps

- (See pages 49, 50, 54–55, and 102 for recipes.)

CHILDREN & PETS

PROTECTION
Keep insect bites, sunburn, and stubbed toes to a minimum

Most of the time a few mosquito bites or mild sunburn is simply a nuisance, causing itching and very slight pain.

But mosquitoes and ticks can carry disease, and severe sunburn may lead to a trip to the emergency room.

Swarming mosquitoes, gnats, or no-see-ums can ruin a camping trip. Chiggers leave a painful souvenir to take home that can itch for weeks.

Be sure to bring sunscreen and insect repellent, but make careful decisions in purchasing these products for children. Not all are created equal. Children's repellent should contain less than 10 percent DEET. Use waterproof sunscreen if going in the water, and apply after swimming.

Follow the directions and age recommendations. You should never use sunscreen or insect repellent on babies less

Sun Protection

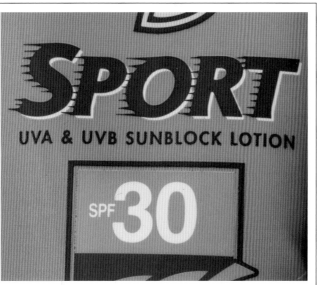

- Use a nonchemical brand of sunscreen with an SPF of at least 30.

- In addition to full-spectrum UVA/UVB protection, look for a physical barrier ingredient such as zinc oxide or photobarrier complex.

- Do not use sunscreen on babies less than six months old.

- Wear sunglasses and hats, and try to stay out of prolonged direct sunlight during the hottest part of the day.

Natural Insect Repellent

- Try natural alternatives first, with ingredients like citronella and soybean oil.

- Picaridin is another effective alternative to DEET.

- Wear long-sleeved shirts and pants to minimize the amount of skin that needs repellent.

- Follow the instructions, including age restrictions, on any product.

than six months of age.

Encourage wearing of shoes at all times. In the outdoors, splinters, cuts, abrasions, or puncture wounds are common if you go barefoot or wear sandals.

DEET

- Sometimes no-see-ums or mosquitoes are so fierce that the only thing that works is DEET.

- DEET (N, N-diethyl-metatoluamide) is proven effective, and most believe it to be safe if used correctly.

- Do not apply repellent to children's face or hands because kids tend to put them in their mouths.

- Apply repellent to clothing to minimize contact with skin.

Wear Shoes

- It's a good idea to wear closed-toed shoes in camp, on the trail, or bike riding.

- Wearing flip-flops or sandals and certainly going barefoot are not the best choices.

- Children may trip, stub a toe, or accidentally put a foot too close to a hot fire.

- The lightweight plastic shoes like Crocs are great choices for camp or water activities.

PETS

Be discriminating when bringing you pet camping

If a pet is part of the family, you'll naturally want to bring it along on the family camping trip. However, you need to be realistic in making this decision: It may not always be the best decision for the animal, depending on the kind of pet and the pet's health.

Most cats don't like taking car rides, being restrained, or walking on a leash. Your pet iguana might be hard to keep under a heat lamp, and frankly, the family gerbil or hamster could become prey!

That leaves the family dog as the best candidate for a camping trip. And most dogs absolutely love being outdoors, hiking trails, sitting by the fire, exploring all the new smells.

Of course, you need to check the regulations before you go. But also strongly consider your dog's temperament. Does he

Pet Gear

- Bring collapsible or nesting pet dishes, food, and treats.

- Bring his bed and a favorite toy or two for comfort.

- A 6-foot leash, collar with ID tag, and waste pick-up bags are absolute musts.

- If your dog tends to get cold, bring his or her rain jacket or sweater and any medications he or she is on.

Sleeping Accommodations

- Bring your pet's bed from home or simply an old, folded blanket.

- Remember—muddy feet on your sleeping bag are not fun!

- Decide where Fido will sleep: with you in the tent, in the tent's vestibule, in the vehicle, or outside?

- The important thing is that you, not the dog, make the decision and stick to it.

get car sick or become a nuisance on long rides? Is he good with other people and dogs, or does he bark incessantly at passersby?

You also need to remember all the pet's gear, like you do with other members of the family. Pets, too, have specific needs.

For the most part, dogs love to do whatever their masters are up to, so have fun making memories together.

YELLOW LIGHT

Be sure to check ahead on whether pets are allowed in the campground, how many are allowed, and if there's a weight limit. Wildlife refuges seldom allow dogs, whereas many state park campgrounds do.

In Control

Most state and national parks require a leash of no more than 6 feet.

- Always keep your pet leashed and under control.

- Never let your pet chase wildlife; it can be dangerous for both of them.

- In places where pets are allowed off-leash, be sure yours responds to voice control.

- Don't leave your pet alone in the campsite; barking is a nuisance.

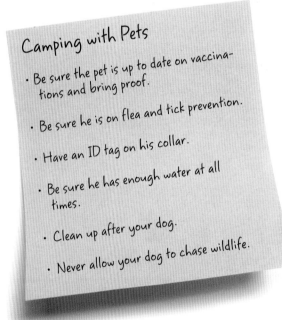

Camping with Pets

- Be sure the pet is up to date on vaccinations and bring proof.

- Be sure he is on flea and tick prevention.

- Have an ID tag on his collar.

- Be sure he has enough water at all times.

- Clean up after your dog.

- Never allow your dog to chase wildlife.

CHILDREN & PETS

153

RAINY DAYS

Be prepared with fun activities so you can make the most of wet weather

You know what the song says about rainy days and Mondays. Well, they can really get you down when you are camping and far from your dry, warm house.

Some of our family's most memorable camping trips—the best and the worst!—were when it rained for days on end. The key is to be mentally and physically prepared.

Do rainproof your campsite. Be sure the tent fly is staked out so it doesn't touch the tent. The worst is getting into a wet tent at night. Be sure tubs are closed securely, or put them in the car. If high winds or heavy rains are predicted, consider stringing a tarp over the tent. Try to create a dry area for the family to play, cook, and eat, whether it's a sturdy screen room or a tarp over

Tent Fun

- A three-season tent will offer protection for playing a game of cards, playing a board game, or reading a book.

- Or just stretch out and take a nap until the rain stops.

- Be careful not to touch the tent walls, or else moisture may come through.

- Be sure the tent fly is staked out so it doesn't touch the tent wall.

Screen Room

- If you have a good, strong screen room, it should provide enough protection to sit under during a light rainstorm and give the family more room to spread out.

- In a wind-driven rain, however, the water will

probably come through the screen.

- Be sure rain doesn't collect in puddles in the room, or else it could collapse.

- Make a screen room even more stormproof by rigging a tarp over it.

the picnic table. Some campgrounds have picnic pavilions, which are great spots to hang out and keep dry.

Bring books, games, drawing materials, and crafts for the kids. Now is your chance to finish that novel or that afghan you've been crocheting. Check the weather ahead of time and have a rain plan. Collect brochures about things to do in the area: museums, visitor centers, a mall, bowling alley, or movie theater. Know when to call it a day. If the forecast shows no signs of improving, and everyone is miserable, you might just pack it in, check into a motel, or drive home. There's always next time!

········· GREEN ● LIGHT ·········

When the sun comes out, remove the tent's rain fly and shake it out. Let the sun dry out any moisture inside. If sleeping bags are damp, hang them out to dry.

Tarp

- A tarp is a versatile piece of gear that can be used in a variety of ways to shield you from rain or sun.

- String a tarp over the tent for added protection in a heavy downpour.

- Set it up over the picnic area to create a dry place to cook and eat.

- A tarp usually has grommeted corners so you can either tie the ends to trees or support the tarp with poles and staked guy lines.

Rainy Day Activities

- Find the campground's common room, usually a good place to hang out, do crafts, do puzzles, read, or get on the Internet.

- Go to an Internet café or welcoming restaurant that will let you linger over coffee or lunch.

- Visit a nearby museum.

- Go to the movies.

- Find the local library.

- Catch up on the laundry in a warm, dry Laundromat!

FUN & GAMES

NEAR CAMP
You don't have to go far to find outdoor fun

When you check into a campground, do ask the hosts what there is to do nearby. Get a map of the campground itself and a trail map if there is one. There may be so many activities right in your campground that you may never have to leave it.

Have children make a list of things they'd like to do in or near the campground: bike riding, hiking, swimming, boat-

ing, bird-watching. Keep them focused on outdoor activities; that's why you're out here, after all!

Based on their age, decide what things they can do on their own and what things you'll do together. For older children (and adults!) it's important to have space for individual experiences and downtime. Don't try to schedule every minute.

There's been substantial research recently on the detrimen-

Fishing

- Time spent with rod and reel is some of the best bonding moments between parent and child.

- Whether you catch dinner or just while away an afternoon, time spent by a stream or lake is never wasted.

- Know what type of fish you might be after so you can bring the right gear and bait or lures.

- See pages 196–97 for more about fishing.

Bike Riding

- Biking is great exercise, and just about any age can participate.

- Tooling around the campground, checking out everyone's site and meeting other children, is one of the fun things about camping.

- If you didn't bring bikes, inquire about renting some nearby.

- Mountain bikes enable you to go off-road onto trails. Do obey the posted signs if trails are for hikers only.

tal effects of the decrease in the amount of time kids spend outdoors. Camping is a perfect opportunity to explore, recharge, and reconnect with nature.

At the end of the day, around the fire or picnic table, share the highlights with each other.

Always wear helmets and watch for vehicles.

Walk slowly and quietly, stopping every few steps.

Bird-watching

- Always bring binoculars and a bird identification guide when camping. You'll be surprised at the birds you can see right from your campsite.

- Pick up a bird list in the campground office, local visitor center, or forest ser-

vice headquarters that lists species in the area.

- Take a bird walk: The best time is early morning.

- See pages 184–85 for more about birds.

Water Sports

- If there's a lake, river, or bay nearby, bring your kayaks or canoe.

- Some campgrounds will have them for rent or loan.

- Pack a picnic lunch and make a day of exploring.

- Always have appropriately sized life jackets for everyone. Children twelve and under should wear them at all times in a boat.

OUTDOOR GAMES
Get the blood going in a little friendly competition

Games date to early civilization and seem to be a part of every culture. Once when hiking in Utah's canyonlands, we found a pictograph showing human figures wearing headdresses and carrying large balls. Goal lines were depicted, and eyes along the sides indicated an audience. We were told the pictures had to be at least one thousand years old.

Games go back much further than that: A 4000 BCE Babylo-

nian board game is believed to be an ancestor of chess and checkers.

Playing games, whether between just two people or teams, must satisfy our primal need for socialization, competition, and camaraderie. But enough of the sociology lesson: Playing games is just plain fun!

Organize a family ball game, or invite some of the neigh-

Ball Games

- Many larger, private campgrounds have playgrounds, ball fields, and basketball courts.

- There may be even an organized game of baseball or basketball scheduled.

- If not, it shouldn't take too much effort to organize a game among campground neighbors.

- Bring a bat, ball, and glove to play an impromptu game of baseball. They don't take up much room.

Net Games

Most net games require only two players.

- Some campgrounds have tennis courts or volleyball nets.

- If you don't have the equipment, the campground office might have some for loan.

- If not, a badminton set is easy to transport and set up yourself. It's also easier for younger children to hit the slow-moving birdie.

- The recreation room might also have a table tennis table.

bors. It's a great way to get to know other campers, sometimes forming lasting friendships.

Of course, it's important that everyone know (and follow!) the rules. If your memory is a little rusty, it's quite all right to improvise with house rules, as long as everyone agrees to them.

Lawn games are readily available in the sporting goods section of large retail stores.

Lawn Games

- Bocce is a traditional Italian ball toss game that is gaining popularity with young adults.

- Tossing an inexpensive Frisbee into the car is easy and can provide hours of fun and exercise.

- If you have a croquet set, a game can be set up on any nice, flat patch of grass.

- If the campground has a horseshoe pit, this is another fun, competitive game to play.

Traditional Active Games

- Delve into your childhood memory to resurrect these timeless games that require no special equipment:

- Tag

- Red Light, Green Light

- Red Rover, Red Rover

- Spud

- Simon Says

FUN & GAMES

CAMPSITE GAMES
Have fun without leaving the campsite

It's always good to bring a few games with you to the campsite. Kids and adults of all ages enjoy a game of cards around the picnic table after dinner. It's a nice break from the routine of nighttime television viewing or Internet surfing, one that you even may take home with you.

At other times, bad weather may keep you in the campsite. It's a good idea to always have a deck of cards or a board game in your gear tub.

Small children will be delighted with the rocks, plants and other natural features right in your site.

The campsite and even the tent itself can become objects in a game of Easter egg hunt. Hide small colorful rocks, shells, or acorns in tent pockets, in sleeping bags, and under the picnic table.

Cards

- Card games appeal to all ages, from matching games (pictures) to complicated Pinochle for adults. Go Fish is one everyone can play: Each player gets five cards; the remaining deck is turned face down.

- Starting to the left, players ask each other for cards in order to get all four of each rank (a "book").

- If the player asked doesn't have the card, he or she says, "Go fish," and the requester picks one card from the pile.

- The winner is the one with the most matches or books.

Travel Games

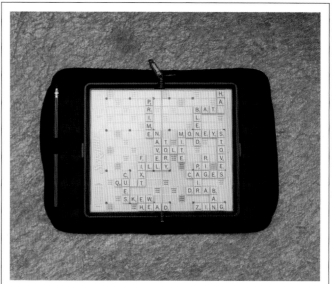

- Look for travel versions of your favorite board games

- Scrabble is a timeless game that also tests verbal skills. Don't forget to bring a pocket dictionary for challenges.

- The Style pictured here comes in its own zippered case.

- Electronic hand-held games are very portable. Be sure to have extra batteries.

Games of the imagination are unlimited and require no special equipment. Search the recesses of your childhood memory, do an Internet search, or purchase a book of games. You'll be amazed how long a game of Telephone or charades can keep the entire campsite entertained.

ZOOM

Imagination games: One camper says, "I'm going camping, and I'm bringing Apples." The next camper says, "I'm bringing Apples and Bananas." Proceed through the alphabet, repeating each of the items.
Name That Tune
Twenty Questions
I Spy

Magnetic pieces are great for car or tent.

Board Games

- Complicated games like Monopoly may have too many pieces that can get lost and money that can blow away.

- Consider a magnetic checker/chess board that keeps pieces from falling off.

- Backgammon sets come in a handy carrying case. This is a good adult game.

- The game pictured here is three games in one: checkers, chess, and back-gammon

Other Good Campsite Games

- Yahtzee is a lively dice game in which you try to build poker hands.

- Charades

- Solitaire (card game for one person)

- Hot Potato

- Cat's Cradle (All you need is string.)

FUN & GAMES

DOCUMENT THE TRIP

Record the highlights in words and images so you can relive your memories later

Human nature tends to forget. You say you'll remember, but after you get home and back to normal life, the memories of the family vacation recede.

Years pass, and you'll find yourselves asking each other: Where were we when we had that great campsite on the lake? How old were the kids then?

Be sure to record the highlights of your camping adventures, in words, souvenirs, and images. Let each member of the family contribute, or give each child her own journal.

Record the dates, places, people, wildlife spotted, miles hiked, and destinations. Record successful recipes, wildlife spottings, funny anecdotes, games played, and people you

Trip Journal

Record miles hiked and wildlife spotted.

- Keeping a trip journal will help you remember all the fun times.

- You can use a regular lined notebook, but if you want it to really last, get one with a waterproof cover and acid-free paper.

- You can download and print your own trip journal at www.koa.com/family zone/tripbook/.

- Use the journal as a scrapbook with drawings, postcards, and brochures.

Trip File

Saving information will make it easier to return to the same place another time.

- Get an accordion folder, preferably waterproof, before your trip.

- Fill it with maps, brochures, menus, and so forth.

- Small souvenirs like nuts or shells can be inserted in one of the compartments.

- Include your packing checklists, favorite recipes, and drawings the kids do while on the trip.

met. Musings, drawings, and meditations will make the book special, as will any scrap souvenirs.

A photograph or, even better, a video bring it all back. After a few months have passed, you may want even to present a slide show to family and friends. And it's always fun to pull out kids' photos years later to embarrass them in front of their friends.

Create your own website to record your trip for friends and family to see. On www.mytripjournal.com, for instance, you can upload photos and create maps and itineraries to create an online scrapbook of your journey.

Bird List

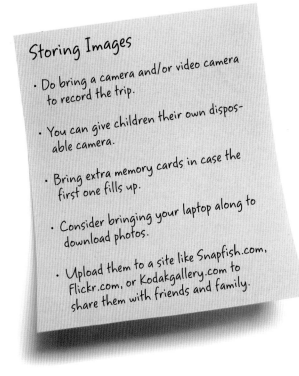

Family Gaviidae (Loons)
Common Loon - Gavia immer

Family Podicipedidae (Grebes)
Australasian Grebe - Tachybaptus novaehollandiae
Black-necked (Eared) Grebe - Podiceps nigricollis
Western Grebe - Aechmophorus occidentalis
Clark's Grebe - Aechmophorus clarkii
Pied-billed Grebe - Podilymbus podiceps
Horned Grebe - Podiceps auritus

Family Diomedeidae (Albatrosses)
Black-footed Albatross - Diomedea nigripes
Laysan Albatross - Diomedea immutabilis

Family Procellariidae (Shearwaters and Petrels)
Northern Fulmar - Fulmarus glacialis
Pink-footed Shearwater - Puffinus creatopus
Sooty Shearwater - Puffinus griseus
Manx Shearwater - Puffinus puffinus
Wedge-tailed Shearwater - Pu...

...mily ...

Storing Images

- Do bring a camera and/or video camera to record the trip.

- You can give children their own disposable camera.

- Bring extra memory cards in case the first one fills up.

- Consider bringing your laptop along to download photos.

- Upload them to a site like Snapfish.com, Flickr.com, or Kodakgallery.com to share them with friends and family.

- Pick up a bird list in the campground office, local visitor center, or forest service headquarters that lists species in the area.

- The National Park Service website (www.nps.gov) has bird lists online for many of its parks, complete with audio to hear the birds' call.

- Record sightings, the date, the time of day, and the weather. These are all helpful for future sightings.

- Most bird lists tell you if a species is rare or common and what season you're likely to see it.

SIMPLY RELAX
Leave some time on your trip for old-fashioned R&R

Don't try to schedule every minute of your camping trip. It's important to have space for individual experiences, to enjoy quiet downtime, and to let serendipity emerge.

You can't underestimate the benefits to mind, body, and spirit of simply lying on your back, looking at the sky. Try it for just five minutes. And five will turn into ten.

When hiking, remember that it's the journey as well as the destination that counts. With children, take the time to stop and look at little things. Encourage their curiosity for minutia: bugs, colored rocks, flowers, trees, and other plants.

Teens especially may think camping is boring. But don't let that attitude force you to try to entertain them every minute.

Do bring several identification guides to birds, plants, trees, and geology to spark imagination and teaching moments.

Hammock

- String up a hammock in the shade to take a nap or read.

- Before stringing a hammock from trees, look for existing posts or fences to use instead.

- Be sure it is secure, or else you'll have an unpleasant surprise when you find yourself prone on the ground.

Read a Book

- Plop down under the shade of a tree, or stretch out in a tent to read a good book.

- Bring plenty of the children's favorites from home, plus a few new ones, perhaps with outdoor or wildlife themes.

- Find out if there are any novels set in the area you are visiting.

- Natural history guides to the region you're in make reading doubly enjoyable.

The outdoor world holds tremendous wonders that individuals often need to discover on their own.

Who knows? The next family camping trip could lead to a great appreciation for the natural world and spark a lifetime of learning.

Lounge

- Treat yourself to a bit of slow-down therapy: Take a leisurely canoe trip on a lake.

- Play the guitar around a campfire.

- Sit and watch the sunset.

- Lie under a tree and gaze at the clouds.

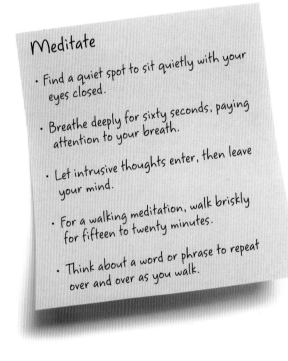

Meditate

- Find a quiet spot to sit quietly with your eyes closed.

- Breathe deeply for sixty seconds, paying attention to your breath.

- Let intrusive thoughts enter, then leave your mind.

- For a walking meditation, walk briskly for fifteen to twenty minutes.

- Think about a word or phrase to repeat over and over as you walk.

FUN & GAMES

TRAIL FITNESS

A little strength training and stretching will make hiking more enjoyable

Whether walking a short nature trail loop, beachcombing, or scaling a peak, hiking is something that can be incorporated into any camping trip.

It requires no special equipment other than good shoes, a daypack, and a watch. All ages and abilities can participate as long as you choose an appropriate trail.

If you are planning on a challenging hike, or if you have been sedentary, it's a good idea to do a little training leading up to your trip. Good cardiovascular fitness will help on those uphill climbs. Strengthening and stretching leg muscles will not only make climbing easier but also will lower the risk of injury.

Strengthen

- Lunges: Holding small weights in your hands, bend knees slightly.

- Step forward with one leg, dropping the rear knee almost to the floor.

- Return to standing; repeat with other leg.

- Do eight to ten repetitions for a set. Do one to three sets according to your fitness level.

Train

Always wear sturdy athletic shoes on a treadmill.

- If you are building up to a long hike, try to walk a bit more each day.

- Train on a treadmill, which can simulate up and down terrain.

- Consider wearing a daypack so you get used to carrying a little extra weight.

- If you need to break in new hiking boots, wear them for a short walk each day for a week.

Pay special attention to the knee, a joint that is most prone to injury yet vital to hiking. If you suffer from arthritic pain, consider taking some glucosamine chondroitin supplements or an ibuprofen before you start hiking.

Remember that the key is not so much how far you go but rather just getting outdoors. It's nice to have a reward at the end: a cool waterfall or a panoramic view. But try to remember that it's a journey, not a race.

Standing Stretches

- Do a few stretches just before you start hiking.

- Stand with one straight leg on a log or rock and lean forward toward the toes with both hands. This stretches the thighs and buttocks.

- Stand with the balls of the feet on a curb, stone, or log and lift yourself up and down to stretch the calf muscles.

- Lift up one knee and hug it to your chest. Repeat with the other leg.

Hiking Fitness

- Be realistic in your goals.

- Be kind to your body.

- Do strength training.

- Increase cardiovascular training.

- Drink plenty of water throughout the day.

- Eat right.

- See a doctor first if you are overweight or elderly or are just starting to exercise.

DAY HIKING

WHAT TO TAKE
Even on short walks, you shouldn't go without the main necessities

Even when you go on a short walk, you shouldn't go empty-handed. At the very least, you should take water when you go for a walk or hike. Staying hydrated is key.

A full, active day on the trail may require more calories than you're used to needing at home. At the first sign that someone is hungry or that little feet are dragging, reach for a quick snack or stop for an early lunch.

To maximize time out on the trail, make sandwiches during breakfast. Place sandwiches and drinks in a small, soft-sided cooler. Or wrap sandwiches in bandannas to avoid squishing them in the daypack. If you use containers, be sure they are leakproof.

Based on your group and how long you intend to be out, there are other safety and comfort items you should include

Daypack

- Wear a daypack with a contoured, padded back panel, comfortable, adjustable shoulder straps, and padded hip belt.

- It's nice if everyone, even children, carries his own small pack to keep one person from having to carry everything.

- Keep water bottles accessible in outside pockets.

- A large top pocket provides easy access to maps or anything you want to grab quickly: sunscreen, lip balm, snacks, or tissues.

Essential Items
- Small first aid kit and important medications
- Toilet paper and trowel
- Trail map and compass
- Cell phone
- Water and snacks
- Flashlight and extra batteries
- Watch
- Rain gear
- Bug spray, sunscreen, sunglasses
- Small bag for trash
- For pets: leash, water, collapsible bowl, food, proof of rabies vaccination
- For baby: diapers, wipes, formula, snacks, blanket

in a daypack or fanny pack.

Terrain and weather conditions may make it prudent to throw in a few more items: warm layers, wind protection, or GPS unit.

In general, be prepared to be out longer than anticipated: A headlamp is small and vital in case darkness finds you hurrying to get back to camp.

Trail Food

Cut veggies, cheese, and pepperoni ahead of time.

- Pack plenty of grabable snacks: durable fresh fruit, bags of GORP, and energy or granola bars.

- Wraps and pitas travel better than sandwich bread.

- Think protein: peanut butter, tuna fish, chicken, lunch meat, cheese, hummus.

- Add energy drink powder to water bottles, or bring favorite juice pouches. Bring a Thermos of hot tea if it's cold out. Avoid caffeine and alcohol.

Optional Items for a Fully Prepared Full Day of Hiking

- Deluxe first aid kit
- Fleece, cap, and gloves if it's cold
- Knife
- GPS unit
- Iodine tablets or water filter
- Lighter or matches
- Camera
- Field guides to trees, plants, or birds
- Notebook
- Binoculars

WHAT TO WEAR

Layer high-performance clothing for optimum comfort when on the trail

Staying warm (or cool, depending on the season) and dry is the key to an enjoyable, comfortable day of hiking.

For a leisurely summer walk in the woods, shorts and T-shirt may be fine. For more serious, high-altitude or long-distance hiking, you'll be more comfortable with technical clothing made of performance, breathable fabrics. These wick sweat

from your body but keep rain out.

Invest in a good rain suit—jacket and pants—rather than relying on a cheap poncho.

If there's any chance of colder weather, bring a fleece, wool sweater, or wind shirt that can be layered. An extra hat and pair of gloves are a good idea if someone gets chilled.

High-performance Fabrics

- A couple of light layers are better than one heavy layer.

- Start with a high-performance T-shirt that wicks sweat from your body. For cold weather hiking, start with polypropylene long johns.

- Wear or stuff into your pack a sweater or fleece and rain gear.

- See Chapter 4 for details on layering clothing.

Pants: Long or Short?

- Shorts are great for warm weather hiking; they're nonrestricting and keep your legs cool.

- Long pants with cuffs that cinch protect from prickly bushes, rocks, poison ivy, and ticks.

- Convertible pants with legs that zip off to shorts are an ingenious solution.

- Avoid wearing jeans: They are heavy, especially when wet, and cause chafing.

In hot weather, wear loose-fitting, light-colored clothing of wicking material. Cover your skin rather than leaving it exposed to the sun. Remove or add layers as conditions change.

If swimming is an option, wear quick-dry shorts or a bathing suit under your clothes.

Your feet are very important on the trail. Wear good, sturdy shoes to avoid injury. Lace boots loosely to begin; tighten them up as you hike.

. . . . YELLOW ⬤ LIGHT . . . .

Cotton is fine for short summer day hikes, but if it's cold or if you'll be under heavy exertion, avoid cotton. When it gets wet, it stays wet and sucks heat from your body, making it a potentially dangerous choice in cold weather. Wool is a better insulator, even when wet, but it dries very slowly. Synthetics, like polypropylene and fleece, are the best choice for keeping you warm and dry. They wick moisture away from your skin, dry quickly, and can be made waterproof.

Socks

High-tech wool blends are warm, cushioned at the heel, moisture wicking, and quick drying.

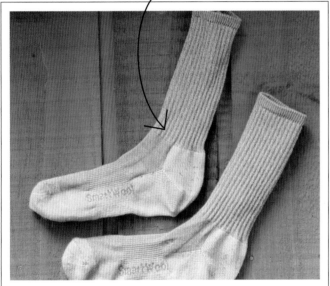

- Good hiking socks provide warmth, moisture wicking, and blister prevention.

- Cotton is fine for around camp and light activities, but when wet from perspiration it causes friction, which can lead to blisters.

- Wear thicker socks with larger boots or in cold weather; wear thinner socks for light-duty boots or in warm weather.

- Wear high socks to protect from scratches and ticks.

Hiking Shoes

- To avoid blisters, break in your hiking shoes or boots for at least a week prior.

- Lightweight shoes, cross-trainers, or even trail sandals are fine for most walks in the woods.

- Breathable materials and vents keep your feet cool, while full-leather shoes can be waterproofed.

- Wear heavy-duty boots with ankle support for more technical surfaces like boulder fields, stream crossings, or steep inclines or when carrying a heavy backpack.

DAY HIKING

HOW TO HIKE

Just a few simple techniques are required when out exploring a trail

A basic walk in the woods or a stroll on a nature trail loop requires little more skill than putting one foot in front of the other.

However, if you will be doing more adventuring than that, you'll need a trail map, a compass, and/or GPS unit and know how to use them.

Most people can walk about 4 miles an hour at a steady pace on flat ground. When you take into account rough terrain, elevation, and rest breaks, 2 miles an hour may be more realistic. Hike by the clock to be sure you have enough daylight and energy to get back before dark.

Keep a steady pace rather than short bursts of energy. That's hard to do with children, so you should always remind them to keep you in sight and stop at every trail juncture.

Navigating

- Get a detailed topographic map of where you are hiking.

- Study the information on the trailhead sign, and sign in to the trailhead logbook if there is one.

- Bring a compass or GPS unit, and know how to use it.

- See pages 190–91 for navigation skills.

Hiking Poles

- Lightweight hiking poles are adjustable. They should be about chest high.

- Poles are helpful and can prevent injury on rocky or steep terrain and stream crossings.

- Consider hiking poles if you are elderly or have knee, ankle, or balance issues.

- Telescope and stow the poles in your pack if you need to use your hands to climb over boulders.

Know how to read a topographic map, hike by the clock, and take frequent rest breaks.

Sip water at every rest break, and encourage children to do the same.

Hike by the Clock

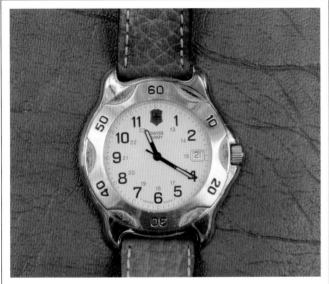

- Determine what time you want to return to camp, factoring in rest breaks, elevation, and time at your destination.

- Halve the amount of time you have and turn around at the halfway point.

- Doing this will ensure you can get back before dark.

- Bring an actual watch; don't rely on your cell phone in case you get out of its range.

Rest Breaks

- Take frequent rest breaks early on to save energy for later on when you are tired.

- Munch high-energy snacks to prevent fatigue, check your feet for hot spots or blisters, and do a little stretching.

- Beginners should consider stopping each hour for about ten minutes. Decrease as you gain endurance and experience.

- Stop for a good break right before a steep incline or technical terrain.

DAY HIKING

TERRAIN

Tricky terrain requires a bit of extra know-how to tackle the trail

Most trails are designed and built with the hiker in mind, going around large obstacles, using switchbacks up steep inclines, and using boardwalks over soggy places. But sometimes there just is no way around a boulder field or steep rocky pass. Seasonal highs might turn a stream that you can easily hop over into a raging river.

There are some specific techniques for handling tricky terrain. But most important is to always watch where you step and to place your feet on something solid, not a wobbly rock.

Before plunging headlong into a technical feature like a stream or boulder field, stop for a rest break. Sip water and maybe munch on a snack while the group discusses the best route to take.

Switchbacks

- Trail builders create zigzags or switchbacks on steep portions of trail.

- Switchbacks help prevent erosion and also make it easier to hike up a steep incline.

- It may look like a tempting shorter route, but never shortcut switchbacks.

- Doing so will create a new path that others may follow, adding to erosion.

Steep Terrain

- Stop for a good break right before a steep incline or technical terrain.

- Take small, slow steps, stopping often to take a deep breath.

- Elevation adds miles to the hike. Every 1,000 feet of elevation adds about 1 mile of energy required.

- Hiking poles help take the stress off your knees by transferring some of the weight to your arms.

You can assist each other up steep climbs and across streams by grabbing each other's wrists firmly. Grabbing each other's wrists is more secure than grabbing hands, which can easily slip.

The important rule is never to rush or else you may lose your footing. Consider hiking poles to help prevent knee or ankle injuries. They take some of the weight off your legs and put it onto your arms and help you keep balance.

Stream Crossings

- Rock hopping or traversing a log will keep your feet dry unless you fall in.

- Wading is often the safest way to cross a stream, although your feet will get wet. Trade your boots for sports sandals if you have them.

- In swiftly moving water, always face upstream and cross diagonally.

- Look up and downstream for the easiest place to cross.

Beach Hiking

- Check the local tide charts or online to time your hike for an outgoing tide.

- It's easiest to walk in the hard-packed sand below the high tide mark.

- Walking in soft sand is very difficult and can cause foot and calf muscle cramps.

- Don't wear heavy boots: Wear sport sandals or go barefoot.

DAY HIKING

SPECIAL CONSIDERATIONS
You must hike according to the abilities of the weakest member of the group

All ages and abilities can participate in hiking as long as you choose an appropriate trail. Many parks have paved trails accessible for the handicapped as well as strollers.

To avoid fatigue, frustration, and possible injury, it's important to choose a hike and a pace according to the ability of the weakest member in the group. Take into consideration everyone's age, ability, and mobility. This can be frustrating for stronger hikers or energetic children.

There are a couple of ways to handle this:

The stronger hikers should carry more weight, whether it's a daypack or the baby carrier. Walk together on flat stretches, and split up on steeper terrain. Members of the group can

Babies

- Use a baby sling for infants or a backpack carrier for age six months through toddler.

- Be sure the carrier has a good hip belt to keep weight off your shoulders.

- This is a great way to take babies and toddlers on the trail, and many fall asleep to the jostling motion.

- Be sure that the child wears a hat for sun protection and that you have all the supplies you'll need.

Children

- Kids often feel more independent when they have their own small pack with water, snacks, and a sweater.

- In the event they get lost, they will have what they need until they are found.

- Children get dehydrated and overheated easier than adults, so monitor how much water they are drinking and how much they are urinating.

- Take frequent breaks at interesting spots.

split up and agree to meet at a specific trail junction, at a lunch spot, or at the end. Just be sure both groups have what they need: map, water, snacks, and so forth. Ideally, both groups will have cell phones or two-way radios.

Plan two hikes: a shorter, easier one in the morning, another in the afternoon for those who still have the energy.

····· YELLOW ● LIGHT ·····

Leash or no leash? Most parks require a leash of 6 feet or less. But some areas, like national forests, do allow dogs to be off-leash. There's nothing more joyful than the sight of a pooch running unfettered in the woods. But you should do so only if your dog obeys voice control and never during hunting season. Never let your dog chase wildlife.

Older Hikers

- More than chronological age, fitness level and medical condition should factor into how far and how remote you make your hike. Remember that age is just a number.

- Do take along any necessary medications and a cell phone to call for help.

- You should have a recent check-up before going on a long hike.

- Be sure to tell those you are with about any conditions, especially heart disease, diabetes, or hypertension. It's only fair to them.

Hiking Canines

- Always clean up after your pet.

- Most parks require dogs to be on a leash no more than 6 feet long.

- Make sure your dog's vaccinations are up to date, and bring proof of rabies vaccination.

- Dogs should wear a collar and an ID tag with contact info (your cell phone rather than your home phone).

- Dog daypacks are available so Fido can carry his own water, food, and collapsible bowl.

DAY HIKING

177

GAME
Wild game is a stunning sight but can be dangerous

Some of our most memorable camping experiences have been the unexpected sighting of a wild animal: a black bear scurrying away from the trail or a tiny Key deer wandering through our camp.

But such sightings can't be predicted, nor should they ever be encouraged. They are a happy bit of serendipity that you just have to wait for.

That said, there are public lands where you are likely to see animals, particularly in the West. For instance, you can see free-roaming bison herds in Yellowstone National Park in Wyoming, Henry Mountains in Utah, and Custer State Park in South Dakota, one of the largest bison herds in the world.

Walk quietly in any woods, and you're likely to see a white-

Observe from a Distance

- Use binoculars, or document the sighting using a camera with a zoom lens.

- Hike and camp away from obvious animal paths, water sources, and signs like droppings or claw marks.

- If spooked, animals like deer, elk, bison, or moose can become very dangerous and even charge you with their antlers or horns.

- More humans are injured by these animals than by predators like bear, mountain lions, or wolves.

White-tailed Deer

When startled, deer raise their tails in alarm, showing the white underside.

- Deer are common throughout North America, even in suburban locales, where they can become a nuisance.

- In the spring, females, or does, give birth to young, which have white spots on their brown coats. Twins or even triplets are common.

- The males, or bucks, have antlers, which are prized by hunters.

- Always wear blaze orange when hiking during hunting season.

tailed deer darting across the trail or leaping gracefully through the woods.

As tempting as it is to get closer to that herd of elk or bison or to try to pet a tame deer, we need to observe wildlife from afar.

YELLOW 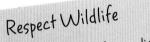 LIGHT

Teach children early on to observe through quiet observation and to never approach, try to touch, or feed wildlife. As stated elsewhere in this book, animals that become habituated to humans eventually become aggressive and may have to be euthanized.

Their characteristic hump and huge, shaggy head are an iconic American image.

American Bison

- The term *buffalo* is actually a misnomer for these large cattle that once covered much of North America.

- They were nearly decimated by hunting, but today their numbers have increased because herds are being raised for meat.

- Although herbivores, bison will charge and attack humans if provoked.

- They can weigh up to two thousand pounds, as much as a small car.

Respect Wildlife

- Observe wildlife from a distance.

- Do not follow or approach them.

- Never feed animals (store food and trash securely).

- Control pets at all times.

- Avoid wildlife during sensitive times: mating, nesting, raising young, or winter.

BEWARE OF DANGER

These are dangerous and sometimes unpredictable animals, so be wary if you see them

Humans have very few predators, and nearly all wild animals you'll encounter in North America would just as soon avoid you.

There are some exceptions, however. In some parts of the country, grizzly bears, alligators and mountain lions are valid fears since they are aggressive animals and their attacks have

been fatal. The danger becomes more pronounced in areas where human population centers are expanding into formerly wild territory.

As stated previously, whenever a wild animal becomes habituated to human contact or learns to associate humans with food or trash, there is potential for unpleasant encounters.

Poisonous Snakes

Rocks warmed by the sun are a favorite hang-out for rattlers.

- Venomous snakes are common throughout the U.S., but their bites are seldom fatal.

- Venomous snakes usually have patterns, but not all patterned snakes are poisonous.

- The ones to watch out for most are rattlesnakes and coral snakes, which live on land, and cottonmouths (water moccasins) and copperhead, which can be in the water.

- Stay on the trail, avoid walking through tall grass, and be careful walking on rocks warmed by the sun.

Bears

- The grizzly bear, found only in the northwest U.S. and Canada, is much larger and far more aggressive than the black bear.

- Black bears are common throughout the U.S., but dangerous encounters are rare. They usually just want your garbage!

- When hiking in bear country, stay on trails and make noise. Some hikers wear a jingly bell on their pack or walking stick.

- Keep an immaculate campsite in grizzly bear country: never leave food out, and change your cooking clothes before going to bed.

However, don't let irrational fears keep you out of the woods or the water. There are specific recommended steps you can take to avoid them.

Below are some of the more dangerous North American animals, how to identify them, and how to avoid them.

If you encounter an aggressive animal, report it to authorities. It may need to be relocated or euthanized to protect other campers and hikers.

Alligators have a broader snout than the American Crocodile.

Alligator

- Several human and pet deaths occur in Florida each year, so this reptile is something to be very wary of.

- Steer clear of prone alligators. They can run very fast. And be aware of the potential of alligator presence when swimming.

- Alligators live in fresh water, while the American Crocodile lives in saltwater and only in south Florida.

- If you see an alligator posing a threat, contact authorities. Do not try to divert it to another area or kill it. It's illegal to do so.

Mountain Lion

- Mountain lions, also known as puma or panther, live in the western U.S., particularly in California.

- Never hike alone in mountain lion territory. Make noise, go in groups, and keep children close.

- If you encounter a mountain lion that stands its ground, do not run away, which only stimulates the chase instinct.

- Make noise and flap your arms to make yourself look larger.

AROUND CAMP
Common animals you may see without even leaving the campground

That cute little chipmunk or squirrel sitting on the fence or the rabbit grazing in the grass can be a delight for old and young alike. And often you needn't go any farther than your campsite to see them.

Help children resist the temptation to run towards animals. Instead, sit quietly and observe. Give children binoculars early and teach them how to use them.

No matter how cute animals may be, never feed (intentionally or by accident), approach, or attempt to touch animals.

That mouse or chipmunk gathering crumbs under the picnic table may seem harmless enough, but it can do damage to expensive gear while trying to get at your food. Never bring

Raccoon

They are easily identified by their characteristic black mask and ringed tails.

- Highly adaptable mammals, raccoons are common throughout North America and can live in northern woods, on prairies, on tropical islands, and even in urban areas.

- In spring, females give birth to two to five young, which are independent by autumn.

- Raccoons love trash and can become pests. They are also known to carry rabies.

- The word *raccoon* comes from the Algonquin *ahrah-koon-em,* which Chief Powhatan and his daughter Pocahontas used in speaking to the Jamestown settlers.

Fox

The most common in the U.S. is the red fox.

- There are more than twenty species of fox, found on almost every continent.

- All are characterized by a long, narrow snout and bushy tail.

- Although portrayed as cunning or terrifying in popular folklore like "Little Red Riding Hood," the little carnivores are harmless to humans.

- They kill prey, usually rodents, with a pouncing technique.

food into your tent or leave it in your daypack.

Aggressive raccoons can ruin a camping trip to the point of stalking you while you try to eat dinner. Their deft hands can open a tub or cooler quite easily and carry away a good bit of food in a matter of minutes. From personal experience, we've known them to steal toothpaste and even vitamins.

•••••••••••••• RED ● LIGHT ••••••••••••

Avoid unintentionally feeding wildlife. Even crumbs become potentially unhealthy fare for quick-scurrying critters like mice or raccoons. During meal prep, avoid letting crumbs fall beneath the table, and use a plate or napkin when eating. Do not scrape food into the bushes or wash dishes under a spigot. Even small food particles and odors will attract animals. See Chapter 7 for more on varmintproofing your campsite.

Chipmunk

- These small, striped, squirrel-like critters live throughout North America.

- They are in the genus *Tamias,* a Greek word that means "storer," referring to their habit of collecting and storing food for winter.

- Their scampering ways and pudgy cheeks have earned them endearing roles in films, including the cartoon series *Chip 'n' Dale.*

- Females can give birth twice a year, typically to four or five at a time, so there are a lot of baby chipmunks around!

Skunk

- This mammal is known for its black fur with white stripes, but you'll surely smell it well before you see it!

- Skunks are notorious for their anal scent glands, which spray a foul odor as a defense mechanism.

- They carry scent enough for five or six uses, and skunks can require ten days to produce more.

- The odor is extremely hard to remove from pets and clothing. Try hydrogen peroxide or a vinegar solution.

BIRDS
Keep your eyes peeled for some unique featherd friends

Bird-watching is a wonderful part of car camping. We've watched hundreds of shorebirds feeding in the surf at dusk and pelicans diving head-first into water from three stories high. We've heard the telltale cry of the bald eagle and the rapping of a pileated woodpecker.

Bird-watching is a pleasure that can be enjoyed all year around. Every season has its own story to tell.

In spring, osprey nest in tall perches. Summer is a time to watch anything from the common robin pulling words out of the grass to the elusive rail clucking in the marsh. Autumn brings migrations of waterfowl, shorebirds, and tropical songbirds. Bald eagles build their nests in winter.

There are more than eight hundred species of birds in North

Binoculars

Consider features like weight and waterproofness.

Cardinal

- You can get plastic ones for the kids for just a few dollars, whereas good ones can cost thousands.

- If you get serious about the sport, invest in the best ones you can afford.

- The optical power is described with two numbers, such as "7 x 42."

- The first number means objects will be enlarged seven times. The second number is the diameter of the lens in millimeters. For both numbers, larger is better.

- The official bird of our home state of Virginia is bright red and easy to spot.

- The medium-sized songbird has a plume on its head. The females are more grayish than the males.

- With the exception of the western states, cardinals are common throughout the U.S. year around.

- They have a distinctive call, a series of shrill whistles.

America, and just about anywhere you are has at least one hundred species. That means you can watch birds wherever you travel.

All you need are some binoculars, a bird list or guide, and perhaps a notebook to record your sighting. Early morning and evening are the best times.

This is commonly called a "fish hawk," although it is its own species.

Osprey

Great Blue Heron

Osprey

- This large bird occurs in nearly every corner of the globe, but the Chesapeake Bay area has the largest known nesting concentration in the world.

- Their huge nests can be seen on channel markers and atop platforms even near human activity.

- They are the only bird of prey that dives into the water to catch fish.

- Like the bald eagle, osprey faced extinction in the 1960s from the use of DDT, a pesticide that caused thin shells and was banned in the early 1970s.

Great Blue Heron

- This huge wading bird is common along fresh and saltwater environments throughout North America.

- These graceful fliers are blue-gray in color with a black stripe above each eye.

- They have long legs for wading and fishing and wingspans up to 6 feet.

- Their rookeries may consist of several hundred nests together in the tops of a group of tall trees.

CREEPY CRAWLIES

Not all things that slither or crawl are creepy and can be fascinating to observe

Scientists build entire careers on studying the world of reptiles, arachnids, and amphibians. Although you should teach children a healthy respect for these animals, encourage children's curiosity rather than fear or loathing.

Snakes, spiders, and frogs play a vital role in the ecosystem. Learning about their eating habits, reproduction, and life cycles makes for fascinating nature studies, making it both a fun and an educational experience for your child.

When you see a spider web along the trail, stop and examine its intricate beauty. See if the resident is nearby, and look at it with a magnifying glass or zoom lens on your camera.

You don't want to get too close to any snake, but it's impor-

Garter Snake

Because of the similarity of the two words and where the snakes are often found, many people call them "gardener snakes."

- Garters are the single most common reptile in North America. They are harmless to humans.

- It is highly adaptable to all kinds of environments and is the only species of snake found in Alaska.

- The name comes from the patterns of the scales resembling a garter.

- Among the different species there is much variety in coloration but not in pattern.

Black Snake

- There are several species of black snakes in the U.S.

- Most common in the Southeast, the black rat snake can exceed 6 feet in length, and it can often be seen in trees.

- They may appear fearsome, but these snakes are harmless to humans and actually are beneficial because they eat rodents.

- The southern black race is another southeastern snake harmless to humans. You may see it racing through the woods after small prey, which it swallows whole.

tant to know which ones are venomous in the area where you are. Watching a black racer move briskly through the forest is quite thrilling.

Check the edges of ponds and ditches, especially after a rain, to find frogs, tadpoles, and slimy egg masses. If you never see them, you'll hear their chirps, which range from a pleasant cricket sound to that of a screaming banshee! Isn't nature marvelous?

YELLOW LIGHT

Never try to handle wild snakes. Even if you're sure it's non-poisonous, any snake can bite. Observe from a safe distance, and learn to identify the venomous kind (see page 180).

All have two body segments and eight legs and produce silk.

Spiders

- There are thousands of species that occur throughout the world. In the U.S. there are only two that humans need to worry about: the brown recluse and the black widow.

- They build webs of silk to trap insects for prey.

- There are many beautiful species, like the golden orb weaver.

- Their webs are intricate masterpieces, especially when coated with morning dew or a frost.

Frogs

- Look for frogs in wet ditches and ponds.

- Even if you never see frogs, you will certainly hear them on a summer evening or after a rain.

- Try to distinguish between different species from the chorus of chirps.

- One sounds like a fingernail being run along a comb: That's the New Jersey chorus frog.

INSECTS
Explore a fascinating, miniature (yet big!) world of bugs

Entomologists estimate there are more than eight million species of insects. Compared with only about five thousand mammal species, bugs far outnumber us as well as all other creatures on Earth.

Insects are extremely diverse, exhibiting an endless array of sizes and colors that sometimes changes with environment. They can be found in every environment on Earth, including the Arctic. But most love warm, moist environments.

A very small percentage of insects are pests, but nearly all have important jobs in nature. Ants aerate the soil. Bees pollinate blossoms. Praying mantis control other insects. Many insects help decompose dead materials and add nutrients to the soil.

The insect world can be a beautiful one, as in the cast of

Naturalist Kit

Put items in a handy little backpack for hiking.

- Encourage young naturalists with a kit for learning about little bits of nature.

- The kit may include magnifying bug containers, butterfly net, tweezers, and identification guides.

- Purchase a nature log or make your own, with pages for recording finds, drawing pictures, and pasting photos.

- A pop-up insect cage will keep insects from escaping until you can examine them.

Butterflies

The black and orange monarch is one of the most common in the U.S.

- There are hundreds of gorgeous, multi-colored species, making butterfly spotting a lifelong hobby.

- These flying insects make fascinating nature studies because of their unique life cycle.

- Look for evidence of the four stages of metamorphosis: egg, larva (caterpillar), pupa (cocoon), and adult.

- Never kill butterflies for a collection; take home only dead specimens.

butterflies and ladybugs. Discourage children from squishing yucky bugs, and instead encourage them to turn over rocks and logs to explore this important link in the ecosystem. Make it an adventure for them that they will remember for years to come.

Bug Collection

- Gently swing a butterfly net through tall grass to collect insects.

- Be very careful of any stinging or biting insects you might collect.

- Examine the more interesting ones in your magnifying bug container.

- Release them unharmed when done.

Grasshoppers

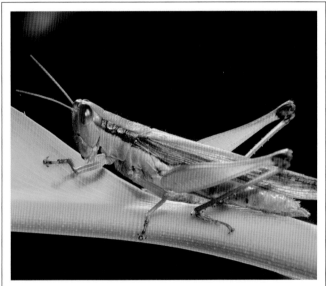

- Grasshoppers and crickets are large enough that you can easily identify some of their interesting body parts.

- Most make noise by rubbing their hind legs or by snapping their wings in flight.

- Their hind legs are designed for leaping, their antennae for sensing.

- Females have two pairs of triangles at the base of the abdomen, used to dig in sand and lay eggs.

NAVIGATION

Never go on a hike without some type of map to guide you on your way

Before going on a hike, first you need a good trail map. Often the park or forest office, visitor center, or trailhead kiosk will have an adequate map for day hiking. A good hiking guidebook should give detailed information and may have a map that is good enough to hike with.

If not, or if you want to do a more challenging hike than the

map shows, you will need a USGS topographic (topo) map that shows trails as well as elevation and terrain features.

Topo maps can be difficult to find. The USGS website lists local retailers who sell them. Serious hikers may want to invest in software that lets you print a map of the exact location you want to go.

Topographic Maps

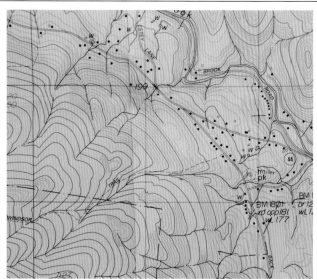

- They are also known as "contour maps" because they have lines that show you the contours of the land.

- Contour lines also show elevation: The closer the lines, the steeper the hike.

- A series of circles indicates a mountain peak. Lines that are far apart indicate flat land.

- Valleys, ridges, trails, and water features are easy to identify on a contour map.

Using a Compass

The magnetically charged needle floating in water or oil points north.

- You can use a very simple compass alone to determine direction: north, south, east, or west.

- You can use a compass that has an orienting arrow to line up with landmarks on a contour map in order to get the bearing you should go to reach a certain location.

- You can use a compass and map to find your position using triangulation.

- These skills, as used in the cross-country recreation called "orienteering," can be learned by reading a handbook, practicing, and/or taking a class.

Having a compass and/or GPS unit is advisable; however, they do you no good at all if you don't know how to use them. You must practice using them before you're out in the woods and relying on them to find your way out.

SKILLS

Coordinates are given in longitude and latitude, such as N25 08.700 W80 23.842.

GPS

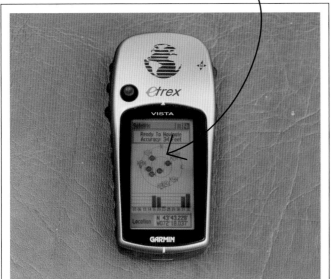

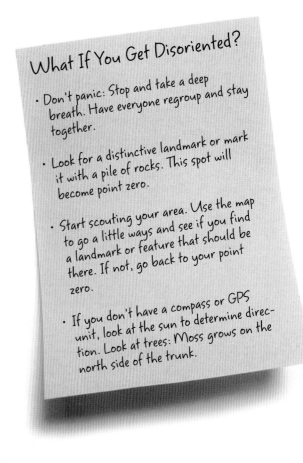

What If You Get Disoriented?

- Don't panic: Stop and take a deep breath. Have everyone regroup and stay together.

- Look for a distinctive landmark or mark it with a pile of rocks. This spot will become point zero.

- Start scouting your area. Use the map to go a little ways and see if you find a landmark or feature that should be there. If not, go back to your point zero.

- If you don't have a compass or GPS unit, look at the sun to determine direction. Look at trees: Moss grows on the north side of the trunk.

- A Global Positioning System unit receives information from satellites orbiting the Earth and gives you the coordinates for your position.

- When you punch in the coordinates for a desired destination, the unit will point in the direction you should go.

- You should mark the location of your car or the trailhead so you can always find your way back.

- Read the instructions that come with your GPS unit, and practice using it before you hit the trail. Always take extra batteries.

KNOTS

Knowing a few good knots saves time and frustration when camping

Entire books have been written on tying knots. Boaters need to know many knots backward and forward, as do climbers, anglers, and other outdoor enthusiasts. For general camping, however, there are just a handful of knots that, learned properly, will make life so much easier. Securing a canoe or kayak to the roof of your car, for example, is one task where safety is

dependent on how well you do your knots.

Some versatile knots, like the trucker's hitch and the bowline, can serve a variety of purposes and are sometimes interchangeable. Practice knots for various jobs and see how they work for you.

Camp tasks that require good knots include setting up a

KNACK CAR CAMPING FOR EVERYONE

Square Knot

Good for binding two ropes together

- Hold rope A in your right hand and rope B in your left.

- Cross rope A over rope B, forming an X shape. Wrap rope A around rope B one time.

- Cross rope A back over rope B, forming a second X.

- Wrap rope A under and around rope B and pull tight.

Half Hitch

Good for starting or finishing another knot; slips easily on its own

- Hook rope around post, tree branch, or pole.

- Cross the short end under the long, main length of the rope.

- Bring the short end over and down through the hole between the rope and the pole.

- Push the knot to the pole and pull to tighten.

tarp, cinching down a tent fly, stringing a clothesline, hanging a bear bag, and tying down gear on the car. The trucker's hitch creates a pulley. The clove hitch is very useful around a pole to keep a tarp from slipping down.

It's important not only that a knot hold well but also that it can be taken apart easily when you need to. Thus, it's good to practice!

SKILLS

Bowline

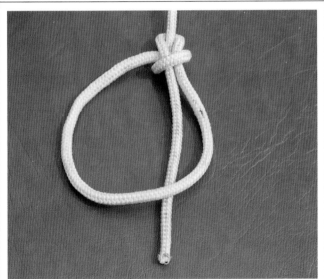

- It's good for attaching canoes to cars or hanging a bear bag.

- Make a small loop at one end of the rope, with the shorter end of the rope over the longer end.

- Bring the shorter end up through the hole, around the longer end, and back down into the hole.

- Pull tight. No matter how much it's tightened, this knot is easy to untie.

Trucker's Hitch

Good for rigging a tarp or cinching down a fly

- Form an eye by twisting the rope.

- Pass a loop of rope through the eye.

- Pass the free end around and then up through the loop and pull tight.

- Complete the knot with two half hitches below the loop.

PHOTOGRAPHY
The outdoors provides the perfect backdrop for great photography

Even inexpensive point-and-shoot digital cameras today are so sophisticated and easy to use that just about anyone can take adequate snapshots of the family camping trip.

The camera you already have may be fine for outdoors. But if you have very expensive camera equipment you may not want to subject it to the vagaries of weather and potential damage.

If you're in the market for a new camera and plan on doing a lot of outdoor photography, consider getting one that is waterproof, water-resistant, and/or shockproof.

After you try digital, the advantages over film are hard to resist. You can check an image right away to see if it came out. You can take numerous shots and try out various settings without feeling like you're wasting film. Simply delete

Camera

People

Get close to your subject and let him fill the frame.

- The term *megapixels* refers to the degree of resolution of an image: Get a camera with as many megapixels as you can afford but no less than four.

- Optical zoom enlarges images. For general shots, 2x or 3x is adequate. For wildlife shots, you may want 7x.

- Beware of claims made about digital zoom, which does not result in good resolution.

- Digital Photography Review is a great site for comparing models: www.dpreview.com.

- To take a good photo of people with scenery:

- If your camera has auto-focus, press the shutter half-way down to focus the center of the viewfinder on the person.

- While holding the shutter half-way, move the camera to the right or left to get some of the background scenery.

- Press the shutter all the way to take the photo.

the images you don't want.

Memory cards are cheaper than ever, so buy a couple to be sure you have enough storage space. Remember to bring extra batteries.

After your trip, you can upload the images to a site like Snapfish.com, Flickr.com, or Kodakgallery.com to share them with friends and family in an online album.

Wildlife

- Use a zoom lens to get photos of wildlife rather than trying to get too close.

- The more powerful the zoom, the more susceptible the image will be to camera shake.

- Get the image in your view-finder, hold your breath, press the shutter, and don't move the camera until after the shot is made.

- A tripod is useful to steady a camera or to take timed photos you want to be in.

Close-ups

- Use your camera's macro setting to get in-focus close-ups of small objects like flowers, leaves, or insects.

- Use the fill-flash feature to highlight detail.

- Set your camera to the highest resolution setting.

You can always reduce image size, but you can never go higher than the original's resolution.

- The larger images will take up more storage space, so bring an extra memory card or two and download to your laptop often.

195

FISHING

A fun sport that can be made as simple or as complicated as you'd like

Fishing is a camping staple that is right up there with eating s'mores. Fishing can be relaxing or highly frustrating: it's all in your attitude. Competitive sorts may get into tournament fishing. But simply sitting by a riverbank can be extremely relaxing as long as you're not on the hook for catching dinner!

It's not a great idea to rely on catching your own food unless you're adept at it and know what the environment will yield. Keep the pressure off, and just go out to have fun, whether being by yourself or bonding with the kids and Grandpa.

Fishing can also be an affordable or an expensive hobby. You can buy inexpensive rigs for the kids to try out. Or you can go headlong into the sport of fly-fishing with an expen-

Basic Fishing Gear

- Rod and reel
- Flies, lures, or bait
- A multi-purpose tool for removing hooks
- A good knife
- Cooler

Spin-casting

A short spin rod is easy to handle, even for small children.

- The line is enclosed in a reel and releases when you cast.

- The weight of the lure or bait carries the line out into the water.

- It uses live bait like squid, worms, or bait fish lures, depending on what you're trying to catch.

- Small children may be happy with a simple cane pole and a bobber.

sive rod, reel, and even the clothing to go with it.

If you don't have a fishing license (required by most states), look for a park or pier that has a blanket fishing license that covers everyone who fishes there.

If you do get lucky, there's nothing that tastes quite as good as fish you caught and cooked over a fire. See page 88–89 on how to fillet a fish.

See page 88–89 on how to fillet a fish.

ZOOM

Practice catch-and-release, keeping only what you can eat. Bring an extra cooler for your catch. Never clean fish at your campsite. The smells will attract animals. Know the minimum size restrictions for types of fish. Get a fishing license if required by the state you are in.

Fly-fishing

- You cast the line rather than relying on the weight of the lure.

- It is more challenging than spin-casting, requiring training and practice.

- A technique is developed that simulates the movement of a real insect to lure fish to bite.

- Artificial flies are highly specific, made of hair, fur, or feathers attached to a hook.

Lures

- Lines, lures, hooks, baits, sinkers, and bobbers: Enter any fishing tackle store, and you'll be like a kid in a candy store.

- Live bait like minnows, squid, or worms can be purchased in outdoor stores and even grocery and convenience stores near fishing hot spots.

- Artificial flies are created by tying hair, fur, or feathers onto a hook with thread.

- You can buy flies pre-made or make them yourself, a skill in itself.

SURVIVAL
Just a few simple skills could save your life in the wild

Despite your best planning, there may come a time when you have to spend a night out in the woods unexpectedly. Causes could include becoming ill, being injured, encountering sudden violent weather, or simply getting lost.

Hopefully you'll never have to use them, but knowing a few survival skills could keep you calm and safe until help arrives or you are able to walk out.

If it's getting dark and/or you have exhausted your options for becoming oriented, listed in the Navigation section on pages 190–91, it's time to hunker down for the night.

The main thing is not to panic. Keep reminding yourself that people have survived far worse than this situation. And you already have basic camping skills to get you through the night. Remind everyone that someone will be out looking for you.

Emergency Gear

- On long and challenging day hikes, always be prepared just in case you have to spend a night out.

- Items to always have that don't take much space:

- Flashlight or headlamp, iodine tablets or water filter, space blanket, duct tape, granola bars, water, lighter or matches, first aid kit, watch, cell phone, rain gear, and layers of warm clothes.

- Navigation aids: map, compass, GPS unit, signaling device like flares, whistle, or mirror.

Emergency Shelter

Rocks can be used to hold the sides down.

- If you are on high open ground, descend to a more sheltered spot.

- Look for trees or large rocks to break the wind: Evergreens are the best protection from rain.

- String a line between two trees with a space blanket or tarp over it to make an A-frame shelter.

- Cut tree limbs to lay over a larger log and climb under them. Pile leaves around you to insulate.

Take stock of supplies that each person has in his or her pockets and daypacks. Pool the water and food and start rationing it. If you don't have enough water, look for a natural source. You can live for days without food, but dehydration comes quickly and clouds judgment.

If anyone has wet cotton on, be sure she takes it off. Put on all layers of clothing that you have, making sure children and older people are well insulated.

Build a fire if you can, create an emergency shelter (see below), and cuddle up together to share body heat.

An important thing is to stay put. Hopefully you have let someone know your plans. Rescue parties will begin looking for you within a certain radius of your last known whereabouts.

Fire

- Build a small fire to keep warm.

- The smoke from a fire may help rescuers find you.

- Build the fire in an open area and fuel with wet wood or other vegetation, which creates more smoke.

- See Chapter 9 on building a fire.

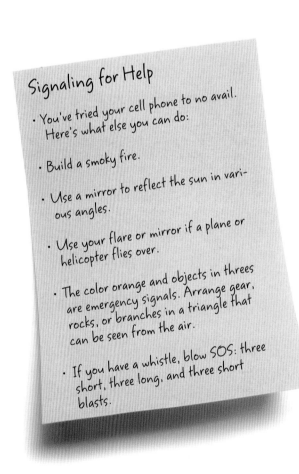

Signaling for Help

- You've tried your cell phone to no avail. Here's what else you can do:

- Build a smoky fire.

- Use a mirror to reflect the sun in various angles.

- Use your flare or mirror if a plane or helicopter flies over.

- The color orange and objects in threes are emergency signals. Arrange gear, rocks, or branches in a triangle that can be seen from the air.

- If you have a whistle, blow SOS: three short, three long, and three short blasts.

FINDING WATER
Water from natural sources must always be treated before drinking

If you are going on a long hike and don't want to carry all your water, or if you find yourself in an emergency situation, knowing how to find water and treat it is a valuable skill. A good map will show you water sources: lakes, ponds, streams, and springs. Often springs and wildlife ponds are even labeled for hikers.

If no water sources are nearby, try descending a ridge to look for a stream. Look for thick, green vegetation, especially willow or cottonwood trees because they prefer moist soil. Even if there is no stream, you can try digging around the base to find a spring.

If you find that a seasonal stream is dry, don't give up. Go downstream to look for puddles or moist spots. In dry, arid land, look for animal tracks; they often lead to a water source.

Water Sources

- All water from natural sources should be filtered and/or purified.

- That said, some water is purer than others: A flowing stream is better than a stagnant pond. A spring that comes out of the ground is the purest.

- Surface water can contain girardia, a naturally occurring parasite that causes diarrhea and vomiting.

- Treatment options include boiling, iodine tablets, and water filter.

Puddle or Spring

- A water source might not be deep enough to scoop out with your water bottle.

- It may be too muddy to use your water filter.

- Use a bandanna or other cloth to soak up and wring out into a container.

If it starts to rain, you're in luck! Set out anything you have that will collect rainwater, such as your rain jacket or space blanket. Look for pooling water in rock formations.

Before you can drink this water, you will have to treat it. See the Zoom sidebar (at right) for more information on this.

Try digging in a moist spot to see if water pools enough to collect.

ZOOM

Three water treatments: (1) Bring water to a rolling boil for at least five minutes. (2) Dissolve iodine tablets in a water bottle for at least twenty minutes, shaking occasionally. To counter the taste of iodine, add a lemon peel or powdered drink mix. (3) Pump water filter/purifier: The charcoal filter strains out parasites; the purifier contains iodine to kill viruses. Place the intake tube in the water source and the spout in your water bottle and pump until full.

SKILLS

Strainer

- Before purifying, try to get out as much of the suspended particulates as possible so they don't clog your filter.

- Pour through a bandanna or T-shirt into another container.

- Or place a bandanna over the mouth of your water bottle.

- Water should then be purified using one of the methods in the Zoom sidebar above.

Snow

Pack pots and water bottles with snow.

- Collecting snow is an easy way to get water, but you'll need a stove to melt and purify it. Rainwater should also be purified.

- It melts down tremendously, so you'll need a lot.

- Bring to a rolling boil for at least five minutes.

- If there are solid particles of dirt, strain through a clean bandanna.

TAKING DOWN THE TENT
Follow camp set-up steps in reverse for this job

Breaking camp can be a chaotic mess if you just shove it all into the car. Or you can take a ritualized, methodic approach. Retrace the steps, and use the same care you took in setting up camp. This will make getting home and unloading, not to mention going on the next trip, so much easier.

It's not fun to wake up to the sound of rain on the last day of camp. There goes any hope that things will dry out before you pack them. Keep wet gear separate from the dry stuff, and plan on drying everything out when you get home.

Try to keep the mood light—and boost group participation—by singing songs, making a game of packing gear, and offering a reward like a hot breakfast in a cozy diner on the way home.

The tent will probably be the first thing you want to start packing. The key is to dry it out as much as possible. The beau-

Take Off the Fly

Shake out any excess moisture from rain or simple condensation.

- You want the tent to dry as much as possible before you pack it, and it will dry faster without the rain fly on.

- As soon as you get up, take off the rain fly.

- If it's still wet from rain or condensation, hang it over a line or the picnic table to dry while you pack up other gear.

- Use a bag to gather up all the odds and ends floating around in the tent.

Stakes

- Pull up the tent stakes while the tent is still erect.

- Wipe clean or knock off dirt.

- Place stakes into their own bag so you don't lose track of them.

- Count to be sure you have them all. Make a mental note of any that are missing or bent.

ty of a freestanding dome tent is that you can literally pick it up, shake out the dirt, and move it to a sunny location.

Take poles apart starting from the middle to reduce tension on the shock cords.

Shake Out Dirt

- If the tent is too large to pick up, use a broom to get out any debris.

- When the tent is dry, stuff the tent into its bag; if it's still wet, stuff it loosely into a mesh bag so it can dry some on the ride home.

- It's nice to let a wet tent dry out until mid-morning. Wipe off any dirt on the bottom of the tent floor.

- If it's in the shade, pick up a freestanding tent and move it to sun to dry.

Poles

- Push or pull poles out of the tent sleeve without taking them apart.

- Hold a cloth in your hand and wipe off moisture, sand, or dirt as you fold poles.

- Dirt in the cord and the joints will wear cause wear and make it harder to put the pole together next time.

- Check to be sure you have all the tent components.

BREAKING CAMP

KITCHEN
Pack gear clean so you'll be ready to go out again at a moment's notice

Breaking down camp takes as much care as setting up camp. Often the temptation is to just throw everything into the car and get going, especially if the weather is bad or you're simply in a hurry to get home. Resist this urge as much as you can!

There's nothing quite as disheartening as carrying a bunch of dirty gear into your kitchen. Worse yet is to discover food-caked pots and pans a few months down the line when you're trying to get ready for your next trip.

Try to take as much care packing up to go home as you did coming to camp. Everything should go back into its appropriate stuff sack, ditty bag, or tub.

Clean Gear

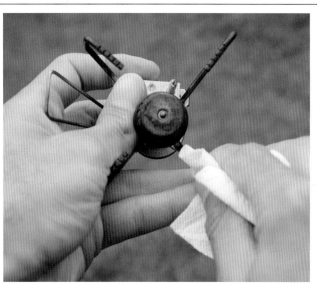

- Clean cookware and tableware as best you can; it will save you time at home.

- When the stove is cool, wipe it off, disconnect fuel line or canister, and fold it up.

- Wipe the vinyl tablecloth or any other items that might have food on it.

- You don't want to encourage bugs or mold to grow on your gear before the next trip.

Pack Tubs

Pack gear and food neatly to be ready for the next trip.

- Put utensils back into their place.

- Put nesting pots and mess kits together and in their ditty bags.

- Make notes of anything you need for next time: spices, matches, and so forth.

- Close food packages securely, and try to brush out crumbs or spilled food from the food tub.

That said, you don't need to become compulsive about it. Going home after a great family vacation can be an anticlimactic, downright solemn occasion. Don't make it worse with too many chores or orders.

Do remind everyone that next time is going to be even more fun and so much easier if the gear is packed clean and ready to go.

MAKE IT EASY

If you want to eat before getting on the road, leave the kitchen take-down until last. Better yet, plan a really simple cold breakfast of granola bars and fruit cups and promise everyone you'll stop for a nice, hot lunch or ice cream on the way home.

If you still have food you want to keep, restock with ice for the ride home.

Cooler

- Throw away any spoiled or borderline food.

- Drain old water.

- Put lunch and soft drinks into the cooler for the ride home.

- If the cooler is empty, you may as well wash it out before you go home to save one more thing to do.

Kitchen Clean-up

- Wash and dry pots, pans, and mess kits.

- Put all utensils back into their place, and put nesting pots and mess kits together.

- Put all gear back in its appropriate tub.

- Wipe off the stove and disconnect the fuel.

- Check cooler for spoiled food, and either clean it out or restock with ice.

BREAKING CAMP

CLOTHES & BEDDING
Separate into what's clean and what's dirty, and pack accordingly

Returning home to a huge pile of laundry is no fun. Dirt is inevitable when you're outdoors, but there are some things you can do to minimize the hassle.

If you've been out for only the weekend, sleeping bags likely don't need to be washed every time. In fact, it's not good to wash down bags too often. Detergents remove the natural insulating oils of the feathers and reduce the loft of both down and synthetic bags. Hanging them to air out may be enough. As soon as you get up, turn the sleeping bags inside out and hang to air out while you pack other gear.

Before you get out of the tent, open the valve on your air mattress or self-inflating sleeping pad. Lying on it will speed the deflation process and give you a few more minutes of rest!

Bedding

Sleeping bags should be stuffed, not rolled.

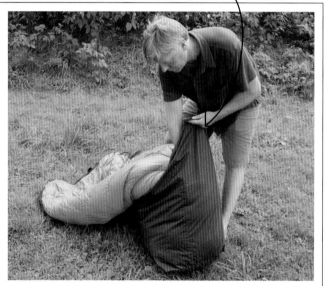

- Start at a corner and stuff it far down into the bag.

- Pack very tightly at bottom to avoid air pockets. The first three or four stuffs are critical.

- Start grabbing by handfuls and stuff all the way to the bottom.

- Cinch the drawstring tight.

Sleeping Pads

- Open the valve on your air mattress or self-inflating sleeping pad, and lie on it to deflate completely.

- Self-inflating pads will need to be rolled up tightly right away, or else they will reinflate.

- Roll or fold mattresses, and place them into their original stuff sacks.

- Let the kids have fun crawling around on the air mattress to deflate it.

206

Separate dirty clothes from clean ones and muddy, wet ones from all the rest. If you get up early, consider doing a quick load in the campground's laundry room before you go. It will make getting home so much more pleasant.

Cleaning off gear and clothing will also help avoid transporting and introducing invasive species to other areas.

See pages 212–213, 216–17 for care of clothes, sleeping bag, and pads.

ZOOM

When packing up in the rain, leave the tent set up until last. Roll the sleeping bags and pads inside the tent. Send the kids to the bathhouse to change to minimize more mud and moisture getting into the car. After the bedding and clothes are packed, take it all to the car immediately so it doesn't sit out in the rain. Wipe the tent floor with a cloth or whisk broom before breaking down.

Laundry

- Separate dirty clothes from clean ones.

- Put dirty clothes into a laundry bag so they will be ready to be washed when you arrive home.

- Keep wet and muddy clothes separate so they don't spread mildew.

- If you have time, run a load in the campground laundry before you go home.

Personal Gear

Put items you will need for the car ride into an accessible bag.

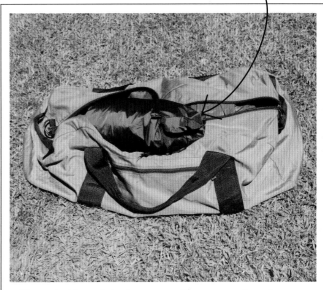

- Try to decide early in the day what you are going to wear.

- But keep your duffel handy for any last-minute changes in the weather.

- Have your toiletry bag accessible for last-minute toothbrushing or showering.

- Put only clean clothes into your duffel. Dirty clothes should be in a laundry bag.

CLEAN UP CAMP

Take out everything you came in with and maybe even a bit more

When breaking camp, the goal is to leave your campsite as you found it, if not better. "Pack it in, pack it out" is the mantra of responsible outdoors folk. Beyond that, it's nice to pick up a little trash that isn't even yours.

Think of the next camper coming upon a campsite littered with food waste and a fire ring full of ashes. Hopefully you have practiced zero impact ethics while in camp (see pages 106–17). But take a look around for any crumbs that were inadvertently dropped, the sock that blew off the line, or tissue in the woods.

Leave things as you found them. If you move rocks or logs for seating, put them back when done. Remove the clothesline or a hammock if you have strung one.

Do a thorough campsite sweep, or several sweeps, to be

Campsite Sweep

- Pick up every bit of gear, trash, and food debris. Do several walk-arounds.

- Replace the picnic table if moved or any rocks or logs you may have moved.

- Remove clothesline and/or hammock.

- Leave a perfectly clean, inviting campsite for the next visitors.

Clean the Fire Ring

- Douse the area with the excess water from your cooler or a bucket.

- If the campground provides fire ring clean-out, you can leave the ash, but do be sure there isn't any unburned trash in it.

- If the campground does not provide clean-out, shovel the ash into a plastic bag and dispose.

- Stack any extra firewood or kindling neatly for the next camper.

sure you haven't left any gear or tiny bits of trash or food.

Take your trash and recyclables to the proper receptacles. If there is none for recycling, consider taking your trash and recyclables home with you.

Be sure the campfire is completely out and cool to the touch.

Dispose of Waste Properly

- Do several walk-throughs to pick up all litter and food waste.

- Dispose of trash and recyclables in the campground receptacles.

- In the absence of receptacles, or if primitive camping, you will need to take trash and recyclables home.

- Try to pick up any extra litter around the site, even if you didn't bring it in.

Campsite Departure Checklist

- Do one last campsite sweep to be sure you haven't left any gear or trash.

- Stop at the restroom for a final potty break or toothbrushing.

- Top off water bottles.

- Say goodbye to any friends you made.

- Check out at the campground office, and drop off trash.

TENT CARE
Proper care will help your tent last for years

After a long ride home, the last thing you may want to do is unload all that gear into your house. Most of us try to eke out every minute from a weekend, arriving home late on Sunday night. First things on your mind will probably be a hot shower and a soft bed.

If you have to go to work the next morning, it may be tough to take care of that gear right away.

Rather than pulling everything out of the car into a pile in the driveway, prioritize the immediate. Pull out the trash and throw it away. Empty the cooler, rinse it out, and let it dry. Pull out wet gear, especially the tent.

Never leave a wet tent packed for long. Mildew can grow and cause an unpleasant odor that will be hard to get rid of.

As soon as you can, set up the tent in the yard, not only to

Set Up

After each trip, try to set your tent up outside on a clear day to air and dry out.

- Wipe out the inside and outside with a damp sponge, especially if the tent has been exposed to saltwater. Never put a tent into a washing machine or dryer.

- Pay special attention to zippers to be sure they are free of debris.

- Spray zippers periodically with a nongreasy lubricating spray (be sure it's safe for the tent fabric).

- Put poles together and inspect for any sand or dirt that will cause early wear. Wipe with a damp cloth.

Seam Seal

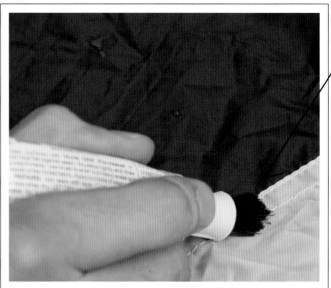

- Even if your tent came seam sealed from the factory, you should inspect and reseal the seams once a season.

- Set up the tent for at least an hour: The seams will stretch so the sealer can more completely fill the holes.

- Apply sealer, wiping away excess. Repeat for a second coat.

- After a lot of use or mildew growth, the tent fabric may need to be rewaterproofed.

- Purchase a spray and follow the manufacturer's directions.

clean and dry it but also to check for any tears and do seam sealing if necessary.

Carefully remove any peeling coating, and apply seam sealer to all seams.

Tent Repair

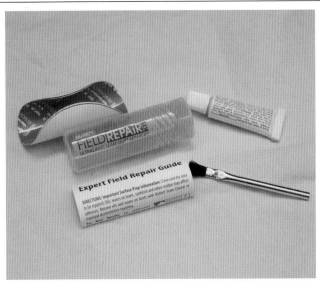

- While the tent is set up, inspect it for any tears or worn fabric.

- In a pinch, a piece of duct tape will hold a tear quite well.

- If your tent didn't come with one, purchase a tent patch repair kit recommended by your tent manufacturer.

- Duct tape can hold a split tent pole in an emergency, but you really need to get a new one from the manufacturer.

Tent Storage

- Stuff the tent loosely into a mesh bag when it is completely clean and dry.

- Store in a cool, dry place out of sunlight.

- Avoid storing in a hot attic or shed: High temperatures can affect the waterproof coating.

- Proper care and storage can help your tent last for years.

POST-TRIP

CLEAN & STORE BEDDING

Take steps now to have a nice, warm bed for the next time you go camping

It can be said that your next camping trip starts as soon as this one is over. Sure, you have housework, mail, laundry, and phone messages to tend to. But don't simply throw your gear into a closet and forget about it until next time.

There may not be a next time if you have to deal with musty sleeping bags and air mattresses that have leaks. It just takes

the pleasure out of sleeping in the outdoors if you can't be comfortable.

Give sleeping bags the sniff test. If they are very odorous, they will need to be washed; if not, then they can go without washing. Sleeping bags don't need to be, nor should they be, washed after every trip. Soap strips natural oils on down

Air Out Bedding

Turn sleeping bags inside out, and air dry on a clear, dry day.

- If the weather is bad, and you can't hang your bag outside, fluff and freshen it in the dryer on low heat setting for about ten minutes.

- Sleeping bags need not be washed after every use.

- Multiple washings reduce a bag's longevity.

- Consider using a sleeping bag liner or sheet, which you can wash after each trip.

Storing Bags

To keep a bag's loft, do not compress the insulation.

- Do not store bags in the stuff sack they came with or, worse, in a compression sack that you use for packing.

- Store sleeping bags in large, breathable bags of cotton or mesh.

- Never store bags in plastic, which can trap moisture.

- If your bag does lose its loft, put it into the dryer on low heat setting for about ten minutes.

feathers, reducing their ability to insulate. Synthetic bags lose loft if they are washed too often. Drying in a hot dryer can be disastrous: The nylon shell can melt, take our word for it.

Foam pads require little more care than a wipe down. Air mattresses and self-inflating pads need a bit more TLC. Follow these steps to protect what can be a significant investment.

ZOOM

Repair any tears in your sleeping bag as soon as possible so they don't get larger and stuffing doesn't fall out. Use nylon or duct tape, cut round, not square. Most air mattresses come with a repair kit of patches and glue in case you spring a leak. Find the leak by the hiss of air. Mark it with a pen, then fully deflate to repair.

Washing Bags

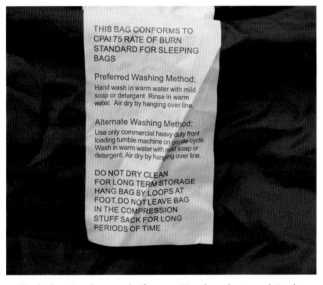

- Wash sleeping bags only if they are soiled, and follow the manufacturer's instructions: The instructions will be different depending on the material.

- Soap strips the down's natural oils and reduces loft.

- Hand wash or wash in the gentle cycle. If the bag is too large for your washer, go to a laundromat.

- Dry in a dryer on the lowest setting.

Sleeping Pads

- Wipe pads and air mattresses off with a sponge and mild soap.

- Foam pads can be rolled loosely.

- Air mattresses should be folded loosely and put into a box or other container.

- Self-inflating mattresses should not be stored rolled tightly. Fold in half and leave air valves open.

POST-TRIP

CLEANING THE KITCHEN
Take care of your camp kitchen like you do your home kitchen

Even if you cleaned all your kitchen gear at camp before loading the car, do a thorough inspection at home before packing things away.

Perhaps you had to pack up quickly or in the rain. Sometimes gear that looked okay in the woods has a layer of grease or grime after you see it at home. You also may have the advantage of a dishwasher.

Clean out the cooler, and leave the lid open to air out. Be sure to put any opened food into the pantry for use.

Clean out any food debris in the food tub to prevent bugs or mice. Restock the tub with nonperishables you use only for camping. This would also be a good time to make a list of things you need to buy for next time and to tuck it into the tub.

Clean Kitchenware

Ideally you've cleaned everything at camp, but it won't hurt to inspect it at home.

- First thing: Empty the cooler and clean it out to prevent spoiled food and mold.

- Run mess kits, utensils, and cookware through the dishwasher.

- Wipe and dry stove and other cookware.

- Store everything in one spot so you can locate it quickly for the next trip.

Cast-iron Care

If rust appears, scrub it off and re-season the pan

- Cast iron can last for generations or be ruined in a single day if you let it soak in water and rust.

- Wash by hand in hot water, not in the dishwasher.

- Place on the stovetop for a few minutes to dry thoroughly.

- When it is cool, reseason by rubbing a thin layer of cooking oil all over the item.

Clean and dry thoroughly all cookware and mess kits, and nest them together in their ditty bags. Place everything neatly into the gear tub, which should be cleaned out as well.

ZOOM

What to do when at home: Unload gear from car and sort. Dispose of trash. Empty and clean cooler. Store food and clean out food tub. Wash dishes and cookware. Stow clean, dry gear. Download photos and memories until next time!

Stove Care

- Many stoves come with cleaning instructions and a repair kit.

- Empty the fuel from stoves with an integral tank.

- Keep connections free of dirt. Use a can of compressed air if necessary.

- Keep rubber connections moist with a little petroleum jelly or lip balm.

Knife Care

- Thoroughly clean food particles or dirt out of the joints of your knife or multipurpose tool as soon as possible.

- Oil the joints and springs periodically.

- Wipe the blades with an oil-moistened cloth. Rinse off saltwater immediately.

- Sharpen blades as needed: A dull knife can be more dangerous than a sharp one.

CLOTHING CARE

Take care of your performance clothing so you can reuse it for future trips

If you've made a significant investment in high-performance clothing, you'll want to take good care of it so it'll give you several years of wear. Never store soiled or wet clothing. It will grow mold and mildew, which not only smells bad but also can affect the integrity, breathability, or waterproof features of fabric.

Today's breathable, waterproof fabrics need special care. Many detergents, especially liquids, can degrade the DWR (Durable Water Repellent) treatment. You don't want a pair of paddling pants to literally start melting in saltwater. As soon as water stops beading on waterproof fabric, it's time to re-treat it (see below).

Laundry

Extremely dirty clothes may need two washings.

- Check pockets and shake out all clothing before washing, especially the kids' clothes. You never know what you'll find!

- If clothes are particularly muddy or sandy, hose them off outside. Excessive dirt can clog your machine's filter or simply sit in the bottom.

- Sort according to color and fabrics that need special care.

- Use the dryer carefully to avoid shrinking or damaging clothing and bedding.

Special-care Fabrics

- Wool: Use cold wash delicate. Dry flat, not in dryer.

- Down: Use cold wash delicate, low tumble dry.

- Synthetics (polyester, nylon, and so forth): Follow directions, but in general, use powdered detergent, no fabric softener or dryer sheets; tumble dry low.

- Rain gear: See next spread.

- Cotton: Fairly indestructible, but it will shrink in a hot dryer.

216

Be sure to follow the clothing's washing instructions carefully to maximize its lifespan. Never put wool into the dryer, or else you'll be passing that shrunken item on to your kids. Wool blends, like socks, may be okay to dry, but read the instructions first.

Also be careful when line drying fragile fabrics like down or wool. The stress can tear or stress the fibers. Instead, lay fabrics flat on a drying rack or on top of the dryer while it's running.

Never use fabric softener or bleach.

Waterproof Clothing

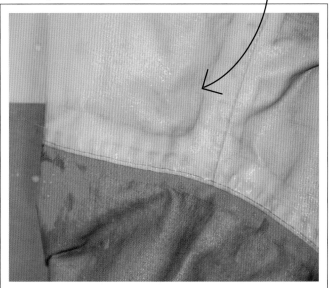

- Many detergents, especially liquids, can degrade the DWR (Durable Water Repellent) treatment.

- If the gear is only mildly soiled, consider simply hosing it off outside or running it through a cold rinse cycle without detergent.

- If you do use detergent, powder is recommended, in smaller quantities than you would use for clothing.

- Put into the dryer for about thirty minutes on low heat to restore the DWR finish.

Waterproofing

- If your rain gear seems to be absorbing water rather than repelling it, it's time for rewaterproofing.

- Use a nonaerosol spray to add or restore DWR finish to soft shell garments.

- Or you can use wash-in waterproofing that works in the wash cycle.

- Be sure the products you use are environmental friendly.

POST-TRIP

217

HIKING GEAR CARE

Take care of gear when you get home so it's ready for your next camping experience

Clean, repair, and care for gear as soon as possible after getting home. If you wait until you are packing for your next trip, you may find that items have succumbed to mildew or even damage.

Leather can dry out, leading to cracks. When properly cared for, leather boots can last for years.

If your water filter was acting a little sluggish toward the end of your trip, be sure to give it some special care when you get home. You don't want to be surprised on the next trip when your filter starts acting up or, worse, doesn't work at all.

Always follow the manufacturer's directions that came with your boots.

Hiking Shoes

Remove laces and pull tongue back to allow inside to dry.

- If boots have a removable liner, take it out and wipe clean.

- Sprinkle some baking soda or shoe powder inside the shoes.

- Brush or wipe soil from shoe's exterior. Use a damp cloth to get stubborn grime.

- Do not dry near a direct heat source. Instead, stuff the insides with newspaper and let dry at room temperature.

Waterproofing Boots

- Some boot brands specify certain products, whether spray, wax, or liquid.

- Fabric uppers generally need a spray. Suede requires a different product than smooth leather.

- Be sure to apply the product well into all seams.

- Allow to dry thoroughly before wearing.

These days the trend is toward replacing things rather than repairing them. But hiking gear is expensive. Many items come with repair kits, or kits are available from the manufacturer. When you can't fix it yourself, try your outdoor gear store for a professional fix.

Most important is to check, clean, and dry gear before storing it in a cool, dry place. The ideal is that your gear wears out from use, not in the closet from misuse.

Daypack

- Shake out any debris or crumbs.

- Wipe off any soil from your daypack with a damp sponge. If it's really dirty, hose it off outside or submerge it in the bathtub.

- Check zippers for debris and treat with a drop of lubricant to keep them working smoothly and to prevent corrosion.

- Open all zippers and let the pack air out.

Water Filter

- Examine for cracks that can let bacteria through the cartridge.

- To clean, pump a solution of one capful of household bleach and one quart of tap water.

- Take filter apart and rinse components in water. If O-rings are worn, replace with new ones from the manufacturer.

- Store filter in a mesh bag, not a plastic bag, so moisture can evaporate.

POST-TRIP

READY FOR THE NEXT TRIP

Always be ready to head out the door by getting yourself organized first

The biggest dilemma for your next camping trip should be answering the question, "Where to next?" If all your gear is ready to go, you can concentrate on exploring what exciting destination you want to explore next.

When you've cleaned, repaired, or replaced gear and supplies soon after getting home, heading out the door will be that much easier. Keep everything stored in the same place so you always know where it is.

Sitting around the dinner table is a good time to talk about what worked and what didn't. Which meals were hits, and which were flops? Revamp your meal choices for next time. What food, utensil, or gear items did you wish you'd had? Per-

First Aid Kit

A good first aid kit should be considered a work in progress.

- Certain items, like antiseptic wipes and Band-Aids, will probably need restocking after each trip.

- Have a good supply of these at home so you don't have to run to the store each time.

- If the first aid kit shows any sign of moisture, leave it open to air out and discard anything that got wet.

- Check expiration dates, and discard expired products.

Food

Keep tub stocked with nonperishable camping essentials.

- Take out anything that's perishable, and clean out crumbs from the tub.

- Leave the tub stocked with unopened nonperishables like hot cocoa mix, canned goods, and oatmeal for next time.

- Make a list of staples you need to buy for next time.

- Make notes on what recipes worked, and discard those that didn't.

haps consider buying some new items. Is everyone satisfied with his or her gear: clothing, bedding, tent, stove, cooking gear, boots, daypacks? If the tent leaked, or if someone slept cold or got blisters from ill-fitting boots, it may be time to upgrade.

Were there activities the family would like to pursue further? Perhaps the family wants to do more kayaking, biking, or orienteering. Consider taking lessons, reading, or training to hone skills before the next adventure.

•••••••••• GREEN ● LIGHT ••••••••••

Play a game of Roses, Thorns, and Buds: Have each person describe a high point of the trip (rose), a low point or prickly challenge (thorn), and something that each person will take away to learn from or a skill he or she will foster (bud).

Keep Gear Packed

- Clean and dry thoroughly all cookware and mess kits, and nest them together in their ditty bags.

- Check your portable camp kitchen to be sure it is clean and to be sure everything is in there.

- Restock spice kit, condiments, and baking kit.

- Place everything neatly into the gear tub, ready for the next trip.

Take Stock
- Make a list of things you wish you had on the trip, and add them to the gear box or the food list.

- Make mental notes of things you didn't use at all, and leave them home next time.

POST-TRIP

RESOURCE DIRECTORY

Trip Planning
Camping on public lands

Bureau of Land Management
www.blm.gov

National Park Service
www.nps.gov
Online reservation system
reservations.nps.gov

Reserve America
www.reserveamerica.com

US Forest Service
www.fs.fed.us

Wildlife Refuges
www.fws.gov/refuges

Private campgrounds
Go Camping America
www.gocampingamerica.com

Kampgrounds of America (KOA)
www.koa.com

Woodall's Campground Directory
www.woodalls.com

Weather
NOAA's National Weather Service
www.nws.noaa.gov

Weather Underground
www.wunderground.com

Maps
American Automobile Association
www.aaa.com

DeLorme Atlas & Gazetteers, by state
www.delorme.com

National Geographic
http://maps.nationalgeographic.com/maps

Travel
The Globe Pequot Press guidebooks
www.globepequot.com

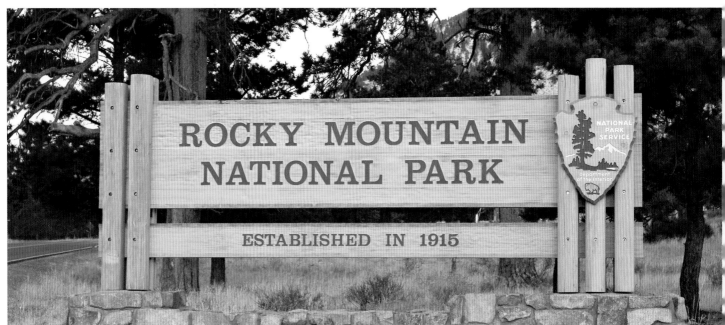

US State Department
travel.state.gov

Gear
Banks Fry-Bake
www.frybake.com

Base Gear.com
www.basegear.com

Camp Chef
www.campchef.com

Campmor
www.campmor.com

Dutch Oven Pro
www.dutchovenpro.com

GORP's Outdoor Gear Guide
gorp.away.com

REI
www.REI.com

Sierra Trading Post
www.sierratradingpost.com

Menu Planning
Campground Cook-off South Carolina
www.campgroundcookoff.com

Jacobson, Don. **The One Pan Gourmet.** Ragged Mountain Press, 2005.

Pearson, Claudia. **NOLS Cookery.** Stackpole Books, 2004.

Packing
GORP's Car Camping Packing List
http://gorp.away.com/gorp/gear/practical-advice/car-camping-packing-list.html

Road Trip America's car-top carrier guide
www.roadtripamerica.com

Camp Set Up
About.com: Camping
http://camping.about.com

Mealtime
Lyle, Katie Letcher. **The Complete Guide to Edible Wild Plants, Mushrooms, Fruits and Nuts.** The Lyons Press, 2004.

Campfires
Smokey Bear
www.smokeybear.com

White, Linda. **Cooking on a Stick.** Gibbs Smith, Publisher, 2000.

Leave No Trace
Leave No Trace
Brochures, books, and online resource
www.LNT.org

Safety Matters
American Association of Poison Control Centers
www.aapac.org
Hotline: 800-222-1222

National Hurricane Center
www.nhc.noaa.gov

National Lightning Safety Institute
www.lightningsafety.com

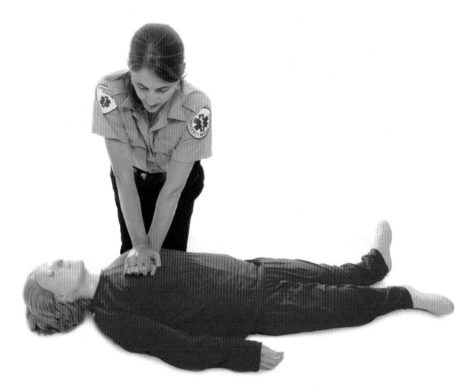

Weather Underground
www.wunderground.com

First Aid
Adventure Medical Kits
www.adventuremedicalkits.com

American Red Cross (CPR and first aid training)
www.redcross.org

Canine First Aid Kits
www.outdoorsafety.net

Tilton, Buck. *Wilderness First Responder, Second Edition.* Guilford, CT: The Globe Pequot Press, 2004.

Children & Pets
Brunelle, Lynn. *Camp Out!: The Ultimate Kids' Guide.* Workman Publishing Company, 2007.

Kids and Sunscreen
http://pediatrics.about.com/od/sunscreen/a/best_sunscreen.htm

Meltzer, Jack and Julee. *Camping & RVing with Dogs.* Desert Winds Press, 2006.

Silverman, Goldie Gendler. *Camping with Kids. Wilderness Press,* 2005.

Fun & Games
Geocaching
www.geocaching.com

Get Outdoors USA!
www.getoutdoorsusa.org

KOA Camp Activities
www.koa.com/familyzone/activities

KOA Trip Journal
www.koa.com/familyzone/tripbook

My Trip Journal
www.mytripjournal.com

Online Photo Services
Snapfish.com, Flickr.com, Kodakgallery.com

Strother, Scott. *The Adventurous Book of Outdoor Games: Classic Fun for Daring Boys and Girls.* Sourcebooks, Inc., 2008.

Day Hiking
American Hiking Society
www.americanhiking.org

National Geographic Maps
maps.nationalgeographic.com/trails

Tilton, Buck. *Trekker's Handbook: Strategies to Enhance Your Journey.* Mountaineers Books, 2004

Trails.com, Inc.
www.trails.com

USGS Maps
www.usgs.gov/pubprod

Wildlife
National Geographic
animals.nationalgeographic.com/animals

National Park Service
www.nps.gov

Peterson, Roger Tory. *Peterson Field Guide to Birds of North America.* Houghton Mifflin Co., 2008.

Skills
Animated Knots by Grog
www.animatedknots.com

Berger, Karen. *Backpacking & Hiking*. Dorling Kindersley Limited, 2005.

Digital Photography Review
www.dpreview.com

Harvey, Mark. *National Outdoor Leadership School's Wilderness Guide.* Fireside, 1999.

Jacobson, Cliff. *Basic Essentials Map and Compass*. The Globe Pequot Press, 2007.

Martin, James. *Digital Photography Outdoors: A Field Guide for Travel and Adventure Photographers.* Mountaineers Books, 2008.

National Outdoor Leadership School (NOLS)
www.nols.edu

Tilton, Buck. *Knack Knots You Need.* Globe Pequot Press, 2008.

Tilton, Buck. *Tent and Car Camper's Handbook.* Backpacker, 2006.

Breaking Camp & Post Trip
Getchell, Annie & David R. *The Essential Outdoor Gear Manual: Equipment Care, Repair, and Selection*. International Marine/Ragged Mountain Press, 2000.

Granger's USA (gear care products)
www.grangersusa.com/products.html

AUTHOR'S FAVORITES

Here are a few of our favorite camping items

Kitchen gear

We've used our **MSR Whisper Lite stove** for both car camping and backpacking for the last decade. It's lightweight, folds up in a sack, and produces a very hot flame. Since the bottle is refillable, there are no canisters to send to the landfill. It does need to be cleaned and sometimes repaired, so take the repair kit with you. www.msrgear.com

Banks Fry-Bake pans are super-light covered pans that double as frying pans and Dutch ovens. Much lighter than cast iron, so we can take them backpacking or kayaking. www.frybake.com

Sleeping

We've been so happy with our first tent purchase more than a decade ago, that we now have two of them: **Sierra Designs Meteor-Light**. It sets up in minutes. We like the three-person so there's room for gear or a dog. www.sierradesigns.com

When the temperatures dip, we're cozy into our **Mountain Hardwear Conness 30-degree** down mummy bag (with a "doubler," see below). www.mountainhardwear.com

A small company with a romance-saving product. It's called **The Sweetie Pie Sleeping Bag Doubler,** a wedge-shaped poly-fill expander we zip into the Mountain Hardwear bag. It effectively doubles a single mummy bag and allows us to cuddle on those cold nights. There's a summer and a winter weight (we got the winter). www.functiondesign.net

Great for stuffing into our kayak hatches and backpacks, but also just for saving space. www.orgear.com

Backpacks
Mary totes a **Lowe Alpine,** women's size. Bill carries large loads in his **Dana Designs TerraPlain.** Both have internal frames.

Footwear
For heavy-duty hiking or backpacking: **Asolo** for Bill; **Montrail** for Mary. Dayhikers: **Vasque.** Around camp Bill swears by **Chaco** sandals; Mary lives in **Crocs.**

Safety
Coughlan's Sight-Grid Signal Mirror is lightweight, compact, shatter-resistant and it floats! www.coughlans.com

We sleep on self-inflating **ThermaRest** mattresses that roll up small and tight to stuff into a pack or kayak hatch.

SlumberJack makes a variety of stuffable pillows that pack small enough even for backpacking. There's even a cushy down one.

Clothing
We love **Smart Wool** socks, long underwear, and hiking shirts. They do not retain odor as much as synthetics. The Smart part is a blend that dries quicker than traditional wool. www.smartwool.com

Rain Gear: **Marmot** jackets and pants. Lightweight and breathable.

Packing
The best gear discovery of the new century: **Outdoor Research's HydroSeal** waterproof compressions sacks. We stuff clothes in one, sleeping bag in another.

MASTER CHECKLISTS

When packing for your camping trip, it's good to make a master list of what you will need. We've helped you out by starting this list for you.

Bedroom

- ❏ Tent, fly and poles
- ❏ Sleeping bags
- ❏ Pads or air mattresses
- ❏ Pillows
- ❏ Ground cloth
- ❏ Tent stakes
- ❏ Sand stakes if necessary
- ❏ Tarp
- ❏ Tent repair kit
- ❏ Mallet
- ❏ Extra cord

Furniture

- ❏ Folding chairs
- ❏ Screen room
- ❏ Hammock
- ❏ Folding table
- ❏ Cots

Kitchen

- ❏ Stove & fuel
- ❏ Cookware & potgrips
- ❏ Individual mess kits or tableware
- ❏ Percolator or French press
- ❏ Small cutting board
- ❏ Utensils: Large spoon, paring knife, chopping knife, spatula, slotted spoon, tongs, ladle, vegetable peeler, corkscrew
- ❏ Can and bottle opener
- ❏ Matches/lighter
- ❏ Pot holder, dish towel
- ❏ Dish soap and sponge; laundry detergent
- ❏ Small trash bags (like those from the grocery store)
- ❏ Hand sanitizer
- ❏ Colander
- ❏ Small strainer
- ❏ Griddle, Dutch oven
- ❏ Cheese grater
- ❏ Tablecloth, napkins
- ❏ Kabob-style skewers
- ❏ Aluminum foil

- Zip-top bags
- Measuring cups and spoons
- Knife set
- Thermos
- Tub for washing dishes
- Lantern and/or citronella candles
- Charcoal or firewood
- Barbecue utensils, hot mitt
- Free-standing grill
- Firestarters or other tinder
- Add your own items:

Water & Food Storage

- Cooler or mini-fridge
- Ice
- Personal water bottles
- Large water containers for camp
- Zip-top bags for food
- Bear bag or canister
- Water-tight plastic containers for food
- Water purification: tablets or filter

Food

- Ingredients for breakfast, lunch, and dinner menus for each day
- Snacks: fruit, granola bars, GORP, etc.

Recipe Staples

- Condiments
- Spice kit
- Baking kit
- S'mores Kit
- Powdered milk, eggs
- Tea, coffee, hot cocoa, powdered drinks, bouillon cubes
- Sugar and creamer (either powdered or canned evaporated milk)
- Peanut butter and jelly, honey
- Dried or canned soup, ramen noodles
- Oatmeal, rice and pasta
- Barbecue sauce
- Packets of mustard, ketchup, mayo

Clothing

- ❏ Duffel bag
- ❏ Ditty bags and stuff sacks
- ❏ Shorts and pants
- ❏ Shirts
- ❏ Bathing suit
- ❏ Underwear
- ❏ Socks
- ❏ Sleepwear
- ❏ Sun hat
- ❏ Rain gear
- ❏ Hiking pants
- ❏ Hiking shoes
- ❏ Camp shoes
- ❏ Bug hood or shirt

For cold weather:

- ❏ Synthetic under layer
- ❏ Fleece mid-layer
- ❏ Waterproof outer layer
- ❏ Hat and gloves

Personal Hygiene

- ❏ Toilet paper
- ❏ Backpacker's trowel
- ❏ Towels/washcloth
- ❏ Soap
- ❏ Hand sanitizer
- ❏ Shampoo/conditioner
- ❏ Comb/brush
- ❏ Toothbrush & paste
- ❏ Deodorant
- ❏ Powder
- ❏ Lotion
- ❏ Lip balm
- ❏ Razors
- ❏ Tweezers
- ❏ Feminine products
- ❏ Cotton swabs
- ❏ Baby wipes
- ❏ Small sewing kit
- ❏ Solar shower

Personal Items

- First aid kit
- Cell phone and car charger
- Flashlight and extra batteries
- Binoculars
- Folding Knife
- Camera
- Bug spray, sunscreen
- Important medications
- Over-the-counter medications
- Sunglasses, reading glasses
- Book or notebook
- Watch
- Radio

Hiking Gear

- Daypack
- Maps
- Compass
- GPS
- Hiking poles
- Water bottles

First Aid Kit

- First Aid book
- Gauze
- Bandages in various sizes
- Wound dressings
- Medical tape
- Latex gloves
- Scissors
- Tweezers
- Antiseptic
- Antibiotic ointment
- Digital thermometer
- Instant hot or cold packs
- Moleskin for blisters
- Sting and itch relief
- Burn ointment
- Medications: Ibuprofen, antihistamine, anti-nausea, anti-diarrhea, antacid, cold medicine (children's liquid or chewable versions)
- Vitamins: Multivitamin, vitamin C, and Echinacea
- CPR mouth guard
- Splints
- Ace bandages
- Disposable syringe

❑ Emergency blanket

❑ Sugar packets or glucose gel for diabetics

❑ Sunscreen and sunburn relief

❑ Petroleum jelly for blister hot spots

❑ Eye wash

❑ Tampons

❑ Snake bite kit

Fun & Games

❑ Frisbee

❑ Playing cards

❑ Bocce, badminton, or croquet

❑ Glove, bat, and ball

❑ Board games

❑ Books

❑ Coloring books

❑ Identification guides for plants, birds, animals

❑ Bug collection kit

❑ Bikes & helmets

❑ Surf or boogie boards

❑ Fishing poles

❑ Kayaks or canoe

❑ Life jackets

Tools, etc.

- ❏ Mallet or hammer
- ❏ Small tool kit
- ❏ Duct tape
- ❏ Fire extinguisher
- ❏ Ropes, clothesline
- ❏ Shovel
- ❏ Multipurpose tool
- ❏ Whisk broom

Baby Items

- ❏ Car seat
- ❏ Stroller
- ❏ Playpen
- ❏ Backpack carrier or sling
- ❏ Diapers and diaper bag
- ❏ Wipes
- ❏ Formula and bottles
- ❏ Food
- ❏ Favorite toys and books
- ❏ Tricycle

Pet Items

- ❏ Proof of rabies vaccination
- ❏ Waste pick-up bags
- ❏ Food
- ❏ Leash and collar with ID tag
- ❏ Bed
- ❏ Bowls
- ❏ Toys
- ❏ Rain jacket

INDEX

INDEX

INDEX